NATIONAL CONSUMER COUNCIL

What's wrong with WALKING?

A consumer review of the pedestrian environment

LONDON HER MAJESTY'S STATIONERY OFFICE

ISBN 0 11 701271 8

Contents

Foreword
by the Chairman of the National Consumer Council

'A walking disaster'. That is, I believe, the way that many consumers would describe their experience of being a pedestrian in the 1980s, based on surveys of pedestrians' own views.

Walking could, and should, be a pleasurable means of getting about. Instead, for millions of consumers, it is something between a chore and a nightmare. We found a catalogue of problems: of intimidation by speeding traffic, of busy roads with no crossings, of cracked pavements littered with dog dirt and rubbish, of footways dominated by parked cars, commercial refuse, shop display boards and cyclists.

Why has this state of affairs been allowed to come about? After all, walking is the only means of transport that can claim to be universal—almost everyone walks somewhere, almost every day. It is also, for many people, the only way of getting about their neighbourhood. Yet the pedestrian is the most neglected of travellers, whose needs are put well down the list, below those of car drivers, public transport users or even air passengers.

Ironically, it is perhaps *because* walking is commonplace that it is neglected—pedestrians are so universal as to be almost invisible. However, it is also the basis for our belief that improving the pedestrian's lot would deliver great benefits to an enormously large number of consumers.

It is time we put our minds to redressing the balance, to putting pedestrians back where they belong, at the centre of the transport system. By producing this report and, simultaneously, a *Pedestrian Action Guide* for neighbourhood groups, we intend to make a contribution to that process.

Michael Montague CBE

Acknowledgements

This report would not have been possible without the help of a great many people. Some were acting formally as consultants to the National Consumer Council. Many more gave their help and advice freely, finding time to share their expertise in discussions during the early part of the research, to comment on the report while it was in draft form, or to fill out our questionnaires. We have set out, in Appendix A, a short description of our research methods, where we also list the principal organisations and individuals who assisted us.

The work for the National Consumer Council was overseen by a special working party chaired by John Mitchell. The other members were Elizabeth Hodder, Lydia Simmons, and Elizabeth Stanton from the National Consumer Council. The Policy Studies Institute, which has done a great deal of research on pedestrian issues, kindly agreed to allow one of its staff, Mayer Hillman, to join the working party as a co-opted member. The research was designed by John Winward and carried out by Jane Taylor and Jenny Potter, who produced the draft report. The report was edited by John Winward, verified by Susan Foreman, prepared for publication by Liz Dunbar and word processed by Eileen Keegan.

Chapter 1
Summary and recommendations

When we step outside our front doors, the environment is dominated by the physical presence of motor vehicles, and we are urged to view cars as the most desirable way to travel—ever faster, ever more comfortable. By contrast, walking is slow, awkward and fraught with danger. Pedestrians usually have to share the highway with vehicles. They are highly vulnerable, enjoy very little protection and, in road accidents, usually feature as victims. Walking is considerably less pleasant than it needs, or deserves, to be.

But the built environment—roads, pavements, towns and cities—is planned and provided as part of our public services, and everyone has a stake in the quality, convenience and safety of those services. For many people there is no real choice of transport, and no way of getting around if walking is regarded as too difficult, unpleasant or unsafe.

In this report we focus on the experience of being a pedestrian in the 1980s. Although not everyone depends equally on walking, almost everyone has some experience of being a pedestrian, and we use the term in this report to cover anyone making journeys on foot, even if it is only as part of a journey involving another mode of transport as well. We also use the word to cover those travelling in wheelchairs or pushing prams, as we believe that pavements should meet the needs of all users, not just those of the most able-bodied and least encumbered.

We have based our findings and recommendations on a series of original surveys of those who use pedestrian facilities and discussions with those who provide them. Four themes recur persistently:

★ pedestrian provision is based on inadequate information about how pedestrians actually behave;
★ there is little proper consultation with pedestrians about the sort of facilities they would like;

★ whenever there is a conflict between the needs of different road users, pedestrian interests tend to come last;

★ laws intended to redress the balance between pedestrians and other road users are enforced reluctantly, if at all.

We are not alone in believing that pedestrians tend to be ignored. Peter Bottomley, as the minister responsible for roads and traffic, described them as the Cinderellas among road users. We hope the pedestrian's story, like Cinderella's, will have a happy ending.

The invisible pedestrian

Perhaps we allow the needs of pedestrians to be neglected because walking is something we take for granted—almost everyone does it, almost every day. While we may complain among ourselves about the state of our streets or about our conflicts with traffic, pedestrians are not an organised lobby, unlike car, lorry or even public transport users. No powerful, well funded group exists solely to promote the pedestrian's interests. The Pedestrians' Association survives on a tiny annual budget and one part-time paid member of staff.

Children are particularly neglected. They are one of the groups who depend most on walking as a means of transport, and who tend to suffer the greatest restrictions on personal mobility when road conditions become unsafe.

When pedestrians appear at all in official statistics it is usually as casualties in road accidents. They make up one-third of all those killed on our roads—the highest single group of road user deaths. In 1985, 1,789 pedestrians died in motor accidents and a further 61,390 were injured. Over half were less than nineteen years old, and a third of those who died were over seventy. These are the official Department of Transport figures, recorded in a particularly conservative way. The true figures are perhaps significantly higher—for example, the Registrar-General's figures for road accident deaths on average run five per cent higher.

Moreover these figures *exclude* pavement accidents—those in which no car is involved, generally caused by tripping and falling over damaged pavements. As we try to show in this report, such accidents are far more frequent than collisions with motor vehicles, and their consequences can be very serious indeed. Yet no one collects statistics on them. We contrast this with, for example, the monitoring of accidents in the home carried out by the Department of Trade and Industry.

A detailed knowledge of what pedestrians like and dislike would seem to be an essential starting point for anyone involved in designing roads and footways, and a detailed knowledge of walking patterns would seem to be an essential starting point for anyone involved in planning or providing public services, shaping our towns and cities, and creating the physical and social environment. Yet walking as a means of transport has received far less attention than travel by motor vehicle, and the needs and wants of pedestrians as road users have been very little studied. Perhaps this explains why the provision made is sometimes poorly matched to people's real needs.

There is an irony in this neglect. The benefits to be obtained from improving the lot of pedestrians are potentially enormous—precisely because walking is so common. Few areas of life offer such opportunities for delivering the greatest good to the greatest number. For a lot of people, walking is the most significant day-to-day means of transport; research suggests that between 27 and 45 per cent of all journeys are made entirely on foot.

It is not, though, of equal significance to all groups in society. Walking as a means of transport is of central importance to women rather than men, to those on low incomes rather than to those on high incomes, and to the very young and very old rather than to those of working age. At the same time, far more elderly people have difficulty in walking. While only about two per cent of the total adult population cannot go out on foot, this rises to about seven per cent of the over-sixties and more than a quarter of the over-eighties. As a generalisation: the more likely you are to have difficulty getting about on foot, the more likely you are to rely on walking as a means of transport—and vice versa. This means, of course, that the failure to provide decent facilities for pedestrians is a significant constraint on the freedom of movement of some groups, and will become an increasingly important social constraint as the proportion of older people rises. Equally, if provisions were improved, people would walk more.

In fact, all sorts of people can find themselves with a 'mobility handicap'. At any one time, their number can be as high as ten million, according to the Institution of Highways and Transportation, whose definition includes temporary restrictions on normal activities. People coping with children (with or without pushchairs or prams), carrying shopping or luggage, pregnant women, those who have had an accident (for example a broken leg), as well as the elderly and disabled, all fall into this category.

The consumer experience

The fact that walking is commonplace does *not* mean that it is without problems. Indeed, the National Consumer Council has become increasingly convinced that it is a significant source of problems for consumers. Our conviction grows out of a number of research surveys consistently showing that the difficulties people encounter as pedestrians cause inconvenience, frustration and even physical injury.

Nearly half the adult population of Britain may experience problems with cracked or uneven pavements in their neighbourhood, according to a 1986 survey reported in detail in chapter 2. Of all the surveys we have conducted at the NCC, this is one of the highest problem levels we have ever recorded. It is also a consistent finding. Indeed we were prompted to undertake the present work by a survey we carried out in 1979-80.

This earlier survey—'Consumer Concerns'—covered all aspects of people's lives as consumers. Rather to our surprise, the problems and difficulties that people encountered as pedestrians turned out to be among the most persistent in their everyday lives. Of the 2,000 adults we interviewed, almost a quarter reported problems simply trying to walk about their neighbourhood. More than half these problems were serious ones, and they affected all age and socio-economic groups—but particularly the elderly, and women more than men.

Pavements presented the major cause of concern. They were broken or uneven, as a result of neglect or building work, often dangerously narrow (or non-existent) or were parked on by cars, fouled by dogs, and cycled on by children. A significant number of people had sustained quite serious injuries through trips and falls. Although many had suffered, few had officially complained.

A shortage of pedestrian crossings was the second main concern. We were told about a number of petitions calling for more crossings, usually unsuccessfully. Even when crossings were provided, difficulties could persist—for instance with the short time allowed for crossing at pelican lights.

The distress and anxiety this caused was highlighted by this comment from an elderly woman:

"There are no pedestrian crossings at all and I get frightened to death with the traffic. I don't even cross the road to my daughter's. I don't go out because I can't get across the road."

In general, the NCC'S 1979-80 survey showed that the declining state of the environment was a major worry to a large number of people. Summing up these findings, we reported that;

"The picture some informants painted of their immediate neighbourhood was grim: dirty, badly lit streets; cracked and uneven pavements presenting hazards for old and disabled people and mothers with small children; heavy traffic; and pollution. People's immediate neighbourhood was most likely—throughout the whole survey—to prompt respondents to say that they had wanted to make a complaint: more than one in ten people saying that they had wanted to complain about their area or any local services. Difficulties walking—the condition of pavements as well as hazards crossing roads—were reported by almost a quarter of respondents. About one in five people reported problems with dirty streets, public telephone boxes, street lighting or disturbances around the home from traffic or trains."

These results prompted us to look more closely at people's experience of getting about on foot. To investigate the everyday problems and concerns of pedestrians in more detail we carried out a further survey of 2,000 adults in early 1986, looking particularly at the journeys people make on foot; the main problems they encounter; and their views on the safety and cleanliness of their environment.

When asked to identify, without prompting, what *they* thought was a particular problem, those surveyed picked out three things:

★ the volume of traffic
★ cracked or uneven pavements
★ lack of pedestrian crossings

As in our earlier survey, we found many people (just over one-third) dissatisfied with the cleanliness of their neighbourhoods.

Of all the things that make life unpleasant for pedestrians, fouling of pavements by dogs is probably one that arouses most disgust. During the course of our work we received a large quantity of mail on this subject. There are around six million dogs in Britain, and between them they deposit a great deal of faeces—often on the pavement itself. Several local authorities are now adopting 'poop-scoop' schemes, under special bye-laws permitted by the Home Office. These bye-laws allow fines of up to £100 on owners who fail to remove dog faeces, for which special bins are provided. The scheme appears to have been a success wherever it has been tried.

Again, our 1986 survey demonstrated the wide range of people adversely affected; in fact, pedestrian problems were fairly evenly reported by people of all ages and social groups. Nor were there huge differences in the level of problems reported by people living in different areas, although cracked/uneven pavements and pavement parking appear to present more of a problem in town, while country dwellers are more likely to have a problem with narrow pavements.

Although the differences were smaller than might have been expected, some groups are, of course, more widely affected than others. People aged 65 and over were more likely than others to report cracked or uneven pavements, bicycles ridden on pavements and dog dirt. Women reported slightly more problems than men, and were particularly bothered by broken pavements. Those taking children to school or day care facilities at least five days a week generally reported more problems, as did people making frequent shopping trips. But on the whole, the problems of pedestrians do seem to affect everyone, and all groups report more or less equal dissatisfaction, for more or less the same reasons.

Ten people in the survey used wheelchairs. This number is much too small to allow us to generalise with confidence about their experiences, although they seem to have a very large number of problems indeed. Other reports have emphasised the particular problems of the disabled. One, published in Sheffield, pointed out that

> "...some people are able to watch the ground carefully and pick out the safest way forwards but by no means everybody is able to do this. Blind people have obvious problems but then, so do many others. For instance finding a safe, even way for the wheelchair is often quite impossible."

We do not believe that the level of complaints received by highway authorities is any guide to the scale of the problem. In both our surveys we found that only a small minority had actually made an official complaint, usually to council staff, a local councillor or to the police. Even people who had had accidents as pedestrians in the previous 12 months were unlikely to have complained.

Pavement accidents

Poorly maintained pavements are dangerous as well as inconvenient. Seven per cent of the adults we interviewed had tripped or fallen on damaged pavements in the previous 12 months, and even more on wet leaves, snow, ice or rubbish. Official statistics are not kept, but it is possible to get a hazy picture of the size of the problem nationally. In 1984, government mortality records show that 189 people died from 'street and highway accidental falls' in England and Wales, and seventeen more in Scotland. Accident and emergency departments at hospitals readily acknowledge the frequency of these incidents, and medical studies have described injury-levels as of 'epidemic' proportions.

Yet for the most part this remains an invisible problem. In contrast to accidents involving motor vehicles, virtually all these accidents go unrecorded—including those that require hospital treatment. This contrasts sharply with the established procedures for recording and monitoring accidents in the work place, and with the detailed information gathered by the Department of Trade and Industry on accidents in the home. Even in cases where people make claims for compensation, no attempt is made to collate the information nationally or, in many cases, within highway authorities. In any case, few people attempt to claim compensation. Of the 141 people in our survey who had fallen over a damaged pavement, only one attempted to do so—unsuccessfully.

To probe the extent of this problem in more detail we carried out two surveys—one by Market & Opinion Research International (MORI) and one among Consumers' Association (CA) members. (The findings are reported in detail in chapters 2 and 3, and the methodology in Appendix A.)

Of those in the MORI sample, about one in five had had a pavement accident in the previous year, mostly a trip or fall on damaged pavements or on wet leaves, snow, ice or rubbish. A minority had walked into overhanging trees, scaffolding, pavement obstructions and so on. Although the overall incidence of accidents in the second survey was lower—at around one in ten—the *types* of accident suffered were similar. Just over half the accidents in both samples involved tripping and slipping over wet leaves, snow, etc; and over one-third (36 per cent in both groups) concerned tripping and falling on damaged pavements. Neither survey included children under 16 years of age, where trips and falls might be expected to be frequent.

By no means all the accidents were trivial ones. Nearly one in ten of the injuries caused by damaged pavements needed some medical treatment, and almost a quarter of the victims damaged clothes or belongings. Those in the CA sample were even more likely to record injuries or damage.

If our more representative (MORI) survey accurately represents what is happening in the real world, the figures are quite dramatic. Our findings suggest that about three million adults each year trip or fall on damaged pavements, and an even larger number slip on wet leaves, snow, ice, etc. Perhaps half a million of these require medical treatment, either at a hospital or from a GP. This is of course a rough and ready estimate, but it helps to put the problem in perspective.

To find out more about the sorts of injuries that can result from pavement falls, we followed up our large-scale survey by contacting a group of accident victims. The injuries they had suffered included many cases of broken bones, facial cuts and lost teeth. One woman had lost the use of an eye. Many had required medical treatment as hospital inpatients—in one case lasting five weeks—and had suffered after-effects over an extended period. Many had been forced to take time off work (seven months in one case), one had lost a part-time job, two people were forced to give up casual work and another had had to give up voluntary work.

If we combine the *frequency* and the *seriousness* of these accidents, a rather odd contrast emerges between the official neglect of pavement falls and the relatively sophisticated recording of road (vehicle) accidents. Our survey of Consumers Association members looked at both sorts, and shows their relative significance.

Accidents involving vehicles are more often serious than pavement falls, but are far less frequent. Almost one in five of those who had vehicle accidents required inpatient treatment, compared to only one per cent of those who suffered falls. But look at the figures the other way round. Because pavement falls are so much more frequent, over *half* of all those who required hospital inpatient treatment were the victims of pavement falls—less than a quarter had been hit by a car, taxi, bus, lorry or motor cycle. Pavement falls contribute an even greater proportion of cases requiring hospital outpatient or GP treatment; in fact they constituted over ninety per cent of cases requiring any form of medical attention as the result of a street accident.

Sometimes these incidents are unavoidable, and cannot be blamed on anyone. In other cases they are the result of poor planning or maintenance. It is important that, where someone has been negligent, consumers have straightforward access to proper redress for their suffering and losses.

In fact, though, few accident victims of any sort attempt to claim compensation. Road accident victims are among the groups most likely to claim, but the proportion who do so is still low, and dependent largely upon someone advising individuals of their rights. Pavement accident victims are even less likely to claim than those involved in road accidents: perhaps as few as one or two people in every hundred, according to our surveys. In many cases, those asked had not thought their accident serious enough to justify a claim, or felt the accident was their own fault. Lack of awareness of legal rights and worries about the effort involved in making a claim were major factors in a large proportion of cases.

Those who are deterred by fear of the complexity of the process are, unfortunately, likely to be right. From our own surveys, local sources and the sparse national information available, we have built up a picture of the compensation-claims obstacle course.

★ First, many people do not realise they can claim at all, and little effort has been made by local authorities or others to publicise this right.

★ Secondly, many of those who do consider claiming are put off doing so, perhaps by an expectation of bureaucratic intransigence, or fear of cost. Some individuals who sought independent advice were positively advised not to pursue their case.

★ Next, many are deterred by the complex system of responsibilities for pavement maintenance and ownership, which can lead to all the potentially liable parties disclaiming responsibility.

★ Even if ownership or responsibility for the pavement can be established, liability may not be. Often, local councils simply argue that the depth of broken slab was insufficient to justify a claim. As we show in chapter 3, letters sent by official bodies to potential claimants are sometimes unhelpful, inaccurate and actively misleading.

★ Finally, if a settlement is made, it is often unreasonably delayed. This is a feature of all personal injury cases, and affects both the eventual sum agreed and the numbers of people continuing their claims, for compensation settlement is essentially a bargaining game which tests the knowledge, skills and nerve of the parties. Each stage involves a gamble: whether the additional legal costs will match the possible increase in award, whether a finding of contributory negligence will reduce the award, or simply whether the case can be kept going, perhaps for several more months, without the cash in hand.

In pavement accidents, compensation claims are rare, and settlements may bear little resemblance to the losses suffered. Information is hard to come by, but it seems that claims are on the increase, and so is the proportion which are met. This is not necessarily good news, however, as it has been suggested that this may simply reflect a deterioration in footway conditions, making it harder for councils to deny claims. We believe that the figure is still only a tiny proportion of *potential* claims.

The aggressive attitude of many highway authorities is particularly misplaced since the majority of people who have pavement accidents do not wish to seek retribution. They are much more likely to want a simple apology from whoever was responsible, and the pavement mended to avoid further accidents. As well as being rude, the attitude of the authorities acts directly against their own interests, for the public can, and do, act as unpaid pavement inspectors. A handful of authorities have recognised this and use a system of pre-paid postcards, available from public libraries and other outlets, for people to report pavement-related problems to them. This is a constructive approach that should be more widely adopted.

Pavement obstructions

Pavements are for people—in theory at least. Too often it depends on whether there is any space left between the lamp posts, direction signs, litter bins, bus shelters, post boxes, phone kiosks, patches of dug-up streetworks, cordoned-off manhole covers, advertising boards, displays of shopware, parked cars, vans or lorries, and, possibly, the odd public bench to sit and rest on after narrowly missing a posse of young, and not so young, pavement cyclists. In short our pavements are suffering severe over-population, and most of it is not of the human variety.

Some of these things can be enough to instil fear, and even act as a deterrent to going out. For those with a mobility handicap, including the elderly infirm, the blind and the disabled, they can also constitute a real hazard. In many cases, legal powers already exist to control misuse of the pavement, but are rarely enforced.

Pavement parking is a constant source of pedestrian annoyance and danger, and was the form of pavement obstruction most often singled out in our surveys. It is a major cause of structural damage to pavements, but the most immediate problem is the actual obstruction of the footway by rows of, often commercial, vehicles.

The law itself seems to be in some confusion, at least so far as light vehicles are concerned, for while it is a criminal offence to ride or drive on the pavement, motorists and their lawyers have successfully defended pavement parking where the prosecution has not proved (that is, witnessed) that the car was driven onto the pavement by its owner. Worse still, some local authorities and police forces seem to have abandoned any attempt to control pavement parking. The major exception was the ban implemented by the Greater London Council. This allowed borough council enforcement officers to prosecute offenders, while the GLC underwrote the costs of prosecution, thus removing a heavy financial disincentive. The scheme was accompanied by a major publicity campaign.

Pavement cycling. Only a tiny proportion of respondents in our survey had had accidents involving bicycles, and such accidents are less likely to be serious than accidents involving other types of vehicles. Nevertheless, pavement cycling does rate quite highly as a source of complaint, perhaps because the bigger problem (as the Pedestrians' Association suggests) is the perceived threat caused, particularly to elderly people.

Pavement cycling is already illegal, but the police do not make sufficient effort to enforce the law, partly because of the practical difficulty in catching offenders, partly because rigorous enforcement would mean insisting on child cyclists using the road, at greatly increased safety risk to themselves.

Building debris, scaffolding, skips, and excavations for streetworks are common obstructions. Broadly, obstructions can be authorised if they are temporary and necessary, in which case they are legal; anything else is not. Skips can be left only with the council's permission for a prescribed length of time. Scaffolding which encroaches onto the highway (e.g. street-level scaffold around buildings) can be put up only with the permission of the highway authority. Organisations representing the disabled have argued that the present arrangements for protecting pedestrians from pavement works are inadequate. In any case, it is generally accepted that they are not always adhered to.

Abuse by shops. It is common, especially in local shopping parades, for the pavement to become strewn with advertising boards and displays of goods—racks of shoes or dresses, fruit stalls, bargain china. These are a serious nuisance and danger to the handicapped—particularly the poor-sighted or blind. They are also, judging from our correspondence, widely viewed as being unsightly and unnecessary. They are also illegal, but the general attitude of local authorities seems to be one of benign tolerance. Genuine complications can arise when shop frontages are owned by the shop-owners and are therefore not on the public highway, but in most instances there is no such ambiguity: merely a failure to recognise the unpopularity and nuisance of these obstructions. Shops and restaurants are also major offenders in using the pavements to dump large quantities of bulky rubbish. In many cases this could easily be helped if the shop owners were prepared to invest in rubbish compactors

In our view the general approach to these problems should be obvious and unchallengeable: that pavements are for pedestrians. Constant encroachments into walking space should not be tolerated. If service-providers and law-enforcers wish to encourage other uses of the pavements, they should ensure that adequate additional provision is made. A much more imaginative approach to the positioning of street furniture is needed, including the removal of all non-essential items.

Police and local authorities should adopt the full range of legal powers available. Although the GLC's pavement-parking experiment was cautiously judged a success, it has demonstrated that the achievement of results is time-consuming and costly. Legal powers must be backed up by the employment of enforcement officials, physical measures such as bollards and parking bays and frequent high-profile publicity. If police resources prevent full enforcement, the law should be revised to permit traffic wardens, and indeed council officers, to bring prosecutions, or impose fixed penalty or fines. The cost of bringing prosecutions could be defrayed by increasing the level of fines—though this would not directly help the councils themselves. We would argue that, in the longer term, a reduction in pavement-parking would partly pay for itself by reducing pavement repair bills substantially. More importantly, it would bring enormous social benefit to pedestrians.

Road accidents

Although we have looked (see especially chapter 7) at the problem of pedestrian road safety, we have not concentrated on this area as it is already relatively well explored, at least by comparison with the other matters discussed in this report. However, it is impossible to avoid entirely. Road accidents involving pedestrians increased throughout the century until the mid 1960s, and have since been in gradual decline. Nevertheless, Britain lags behind other comparable countries in pedestrian safety. In terms of pedestrian deaths per 100,000 population we rate well below the Netherlands, Sweden, Japan and Norway, for example—running neck and neck with the German Democratic Republic.

Quite apart from the human tragedy, accidents also impose an economic cost on victims, on relatives and on society. The Department of Transport tries to calculate these costs, taking account of factors such as loss of economic output, hospital treatment, police and administration, and a notional calculation of pain, suffering and grief caused by death or injury.

In 1984 their *average* figure for pedestrians killed or injured was £6,960. This is higher than for any other category of road-user, reflecting the greater likelihood of death among pedestrians. Recent research has suggested that present methods of costing are likely to be underestimates.

The intimidation caused by road traffic contributes to the unpleasantness of being a pedestrian. We have already noted that it was a major cause of spontaneously expressed dissatisfaction in the NCC's own 1979/80 survey, and this is supported by work published in 1980 by the Office of Population Censuses and Surveys, which found that over half of their sample considered road-crossing to be more difficult than five years previously. Overwhelmingly, this was blamed on increases in both the volume of traffic and its speed.

Ideally, pedestrians should be able to make their journeys without intimidation or risk to life and limb, and should not suffer restrictions on their movement or convenience as a price of improved safety. Realistically, public highways have to cater for all kinds of transport, and conflicts are bound to arise. We believe that pedestrians should be able to expect at least equal consideration when such conflicts are being addressed. This is especially true of safety measures, simply because pedestrians are the most vulnerable of road users. At present, pedestrians are seriously neglected. We do not pretend that their position can be improved without cost to the *convenience* of other road-users, but we do believe that the *safety* of others need not suffer.

Our focus on the status of pedestrians is an important one, for there is no shortage of proven engineering and traffic management measures which could substantially improve pedestrian safety. Many are already in operation in this country and abroad. It is therefore surprising and disconcerting that progress has been so slow. Some of the main obstacles are created by central government. The principal ones are a failure to encourage the adoption of small-scale, low-cost measures or to provide funding incentives for local authorities, and over-restrictive regulation of measures like road humps and traffic signals with pedestrian phases, which both prevents local authorities from meeting the demands of local people and stifles experiment. Of course, central government is not solely to blame—too low a priority has been given to these measures by local authorities themselves. Even if safety schemes *are* implemented, they may be undermined by inadequate enforcement. As with pavement parking, there is often an unwillingness on the part of the police to enforce the laws that do exist, especially those on speeding. We hope that the new system of fixed-penalty fines will encourage a more active enforcement policy.

As well as physical measures, there is a need to raise the general level of consciousness about pedestrian safety at all levels. More research is needed into the circumstances of pedestrian accidents, to help local authorities plan improvements. Skimping on research is a substantial false economy if it leads to the adoption of ineffectual measures. Drivers need far more specific education about their responsibilities towards other road-users, especially pedestrians, and some demonstration of this should be incorporated into the driving test. It should also be given greater emphasis in the Highway Code, in Department of Transport advertising and in the 'Driving' manual. Road safety education should be more integrated in the school and college curriculum. A National Traffic Club should be established for pre-school children (based on the Scandinavian and GLC/TRRL experience). The Department of Transport should take a lead in disseminating information about novel road safety schemes.

Planning for pedestrians

If facilities for the pedestrian are to be improved significantly, they must be given a much higher priority from the outset—in other words they must have a central place in the planning process. Provision for pedestrians does not usually involve major engineering projects, and for this very reason can easily be overlooked, though the creation of a first-class pedestrian environment is certainly a demanding, complex and challenging task. We believe that pedestrians' interests should be put at the centre of both transport and land use planning.

In some places, of course, a great deal is already being done—town centres are being pedestrianised, new housing estates that are safe for pedestrians are being built, pavement surfaces are being developed to aid people with mobility handicaps, and so on. However welcome, though, such improvements are far from universal, and do not constitute evidence of a willingness to treat pedestrians and cars as equals.

Indeed, the whole trend of planning policies is to make access on foot more difficult. In deciding the size and location of facilities like hospitals and shopping centres, attention has focused on the economies of scale that can be achieved by building bigger and bigger units. Although this improves efficiency, it also reduces ease of access—particularly for those without a car. The trend has been adopted in both the public sector (hospitals and schools) and the private sector (hypermarkets and shopping centres). New facilities are designed primarily for those with access to cars, and offer that group a privileged service. People without cars are, at best, denied the advantages of the newest facilities, and may even suffer an overall reduction in opportunities as older, smaller units are closed. Children are, once again, among the groups most disadvantaged by this trend.

The failure to give pedestrians proper weight in transport planning can produce conditions that are inconvenient, unpleasant, unsafe or insecure. At its most dramatic, bad road planning can lead to what is known as 'community severance'—when neighbourhoods are cut in half by busy traffic routes. An outstanding illustration of this is London's North Circular Road.

Transport plans are one obvious place for addressing the question of pedestrian provision. Indeed, central government has already asked highway authorities to include specific plans, but so far the response seems to be disappointing.

Structure plans are required to discuss measures to improve the physical environment and for traffic management, and therefore should, in principle, already include pedestrians. In practice, they rarely do. We believe that structure plans should include specific policies for pedestrians, in order to improve their status in the overall planning process. As these plans must be approved by the Secretary of State, central government could give the lead. Local plans are perhaps even more important, for it is at this level that pedestrian facilities must actually be provided. The NCC has been shown several good examples of plans that pay great attention to pedestrians, but we fear that these tend to be the exception rather than the rule.

We have detected two main reasons for this. First, councils rarely seem to collect information from pedestrians themselves. Secondly, there seems to be little attempt to develop strategies for pedestrian movement that aim to produce a properly integrated network. The need for proper consultation is a major theme in our suggested approach.

Of course, consultation in a formal sense is already built into the system—it is required by the Town and Country Planning Acts. Many local authorities have found the process to be an unhappy one. Some highway planning inquiries have turned into lengthy, bitter battles. In other cases, authorities have found it difficult to gain the participation of a significant proportion of the public. This does not lessen the need for consultation. Other local authorities have made a success of it, and providers of public services must find ways of involving the users in the design process. We quote with approval the view of one planner:

> "If you wish to design enjoyment into a pedestrian journey, then ask the pedestrian what he thinks about it. Research what you have—design and implement then research again. Any other consumer product would be treated in this way..."

If consulting procedures are failing, they should be improved, not further neglected.

We believe that the single most significant improvement would be a recognition that planners should be designing *with* the people, not for them. This includes the recognition that planning must take account of people's perceptions as well as 'objective' facts, and that these two things may well conflict. For example, a safe environment may not necessarily be a very convenient one. Engineers should not be so surprised when people ignore the underpass or footbridge they have designed, preferring instead to dodge between the speeding cars on the road itself.

The greatest opportunities for improvements at the planning stage obviously apply to green field projects. Existing sites are more limiting, but there is still plenty that can be—and is being—done. The options include pedestrianisation of town centres; traffic management schemes, pedestrian priority routes, the provision of amenity routes and pavement widening. Measures to improve walking conditions for people with mobility handicaps include dropped kerbs, tactile surfaces, network routes, wheelchair clearways and so on.

Although the main responsibility rests with local service providers, we believe that central government must also play its part. At the very least, ministers and officials must ensure that pedestrians are properly considered in transport policies and in structure plans. Most importantly, it must ensure that sufficient funds are available to turn these plans into reality. Redressing the low status that has been given to pedestrians is, in the end, a matter of political will.

What is to be done?

Measures to improve the lot of pedestrians are of very different kinds, requiring expertise in the law, planning, engineering, traffic management, and design. We are not experts in all these fields, and cannot pretend to have the definitive answer to all the problems we reveal. Nevertheless, we have tried to suggest detailed solutions wherever possible, and we hope that these will be considered, and constructively criticised, by those who do have expertise. Our approach throughout has been to examine the problems from the viewpoint of pedestrians themselves, looking through their eyes and learning from their experiences. Sometimes the conclusions are unavoidable. For example, consumer views about the condition of pavements suggest that they are a national disgrace, responsible for a huge, uncatalogued number of pedestrian accidents. Expenditure priorities must be revised. At other times the way forward is not so clear and we must leave to others the resolution of the problems we reveal.

We set out our detailed recommendations in chapter 8. The main thrust of our report can be summarised as follows.

★ *Most importantly, we are calling for a change of priority in assessing the needs of all road users, putting pedestrian needs at the centre of transport policy.*

The NCC is not anti-motorist—cars provide enormous benefits of personal mobility to a very large number of people—but planning for cars can lead to pedestrians being pushed to the margins, both literally and figuratively. It is rare for pedestrians' safety, convenience or pleasure to take precedence over those of other road users.

★ *The interests of pedestrians should also be put at the centre of the planning process.*

Very few local authorities produce strategic plans for pedestrian movement. Yet two major trends in planning are having a major impact on pedestrians. Location policies are leading to the concentration of essential services, making it increasingly difficult to reach them on foot. The amalgamation or closure of schools, hospitals, post offices, local shops and so on, and the development of large-scale shopping centres (often outside the town centre) can severely restrict access for those who rely on walking as their main means of getting about. At the same time, more and more towns are creating 'pedestrianised' areas. While this *can* be of great benefit to the pedestrian, done badly it simply produces pockets of pedestrianisation that fail to form a network.

There are welcome signs that this piecemeal approach is being replaced by one that looks at the needs of a whole area. To ensure that this progress continues, we make four specific suggestions: that all local planning authorities should be required to produce pedestrian movement plans; that 'pedestrian impact statements' should be prepared for all major new developments; that transport plans produced by county and regional councils should deal much more thoroughly with provision for pedestrians; and that both the upper and lower tiers of local government should create 'pedestrian units' to take responsibility for these plans and to oversee pedestrian safety in their area. Nothing concentrates the mind more than giving someone a particular problem to solve. We would also like to see a pedestrian unit set up within the Department of Transport, to co-ordinate the work being carried out by its own various divisions, and by those in the Department of the Environment.

★ *Much more information on the needs and preferences of pedestrians should be collected.*

As part of the general neglect of pedestrians, what little planning is done for them often takes place in an information vacuum. Research is needed, both nationally and locally, to collect more data on who is walking where and for what purpose. Without this sort of basic information planners cannot be sure that they are meeting the real needs of pedestrians, while crucial areas of policy—including accident prevention measures—will fail to take full account of the behaviour and circumstances of pedestrians. If the needs of pedestrians are properly researched and quantified, they will be more difficult to overlook. At present, there does not even seem to be a national (or, in many cases, local) inventory of pavements, so how can politicians allocate resources in a sensible way?

★ *Allied to this is our next conclusion: that service planners and providers should develop much better means of communication and consultation with the people for whom they are providing services.*

It appears that some local authorities fail to carry out even the most rudimentary analysis of the complaints they receive from the public about pedestrian matters. Yet pedestrians (and cyclists) can act as unpaid highway inspectors if they are encouraged to report the problems they find. Equally, planners too often try to impose their own solutions, rather than seeking the users' views on the environment in which they want to live. Consultation and communication should involve a continuing dialogue, in which both sides listen to what the other has to say.

★ *Action must be taken to reduce the number of accidents caused by damaged pavements, and to improve redress for people who suffer injury or damage.*

This appears to be a seriously neglected area. Our research suggests that accidents caused by tripping or falling on damaged pavements constitute a major problem, and we would like to see more evidence collected nationally and locally on their true extent. The first priority must of course, be to improve the conditions of the pavement. This involves improving the level of maintenance, minimising the effects of public utilities' streetworks, and preventing vehicles from damaging the surface of the footway. When accidents do occur, local authorities and others such as advice centres should make sure that pedestrians are informed about their rights to claim compensation and helped through the legal process.

★ *We would like to see much tougher action taken against all the things that make life difficult, dangerous, inconvenient or unpleasant for pedestrians.*

Dangerous driving is a particular problem but we would also single out pavement parking, unguarded street works, cycling on pavements where it constitutes a danger to pedestrians, pavement obstructions, littering (though pedestrians themselves will often be to blame), and dog dirt.

In certain cases, the law itself needs strengthening. For example, a general ban on pavement parking exists on the statute book but has never been brought into force. More often, existing laws need to be better enforced, especially those concerning motorists. Chief police constables have wide discretion over the setting of their own priorities for enforcement, and dealing with traffic offenders generally seems to come near the bottom of the list.

★ *Pedestrian interests need to be given a higher political priority.*

In many cases the means to improve conditions for pedestrians already exist—what is lacking is the political will. Almost all the people we spoke to during our investigations impressed us with their concern for pedestrians, and most accepted that progress was too slow. However, this failure was always blamed on someone else; central government, for example, for not providing enough money or clear guidance on priorities; highway authorities for being too keen on cars and roads rather than on people; the police for failing to take a tougher stand. Planners blame engineers, county/regional councils and district councils blame each other, and everyone has a crack at pedestrians for illogically valuing their convenience more highly than their safety.

Responsibility for providing pedestrian facilities appears to be hopelessly fragmented. Local authorities have the major responsibility, but their freedom of action—and access to resources—is limited. The division of responsibility between upper and lower tiers of local government can be a further barrier, for it is generally the upper tier which rations the cash, while most pedestrian journeys are very local in nature.

If things are to change, pressure must be applied from both ends— both 'downwards' from central government and 'upwards' from pedestrians and local people themselves. Politicians, who control the sharing out of resources, must be convinced that people care about their pavements and their safety on the roads. This is why, at the same time as publishing this report, we are issuing an action guide for pedestrians themselves. We hope that this will help them to assess local conditions for themselves and to press for any necessary improvements. The guide is like a tool kit, to give people the means and the skills to create a better environment.

★ *Finally, all our recommendations point to the need for a clear sense of direction to be given by central government.*

Statements from ministers, and our discussions with officials at the Departments of Transport and Environment, suggest that parts of government at least are beginning to make the right noises. There is evident concern for the safety of pedestrians on the roads, and for issues such as personal security and the condition of our environment. This concern must be translated into government action of two kinds: first, guidance in the setting of priorities—although we believe that the actual implementation of policies should remain in the hands of local government and, secondly, making sure that enough money is provided to give these policies a chance.

Chapter 2
The views of pedestrians

We report here the results of two surveys carried out for the National Consumer Council, both of which measured public feeling about the condition of pavements and the provisions made for pedestrians. This chapter concentrates in broad terms on people's experiences as pedestrians, and the problems they face. In chapter 3 we focus on pavement accidents, and at what happens to pedestrians who try to claim compensation.

The first—which we called the 'Consumer Concerns Survey'—was carried out in 1979-80, and involved interviews with nearly 2,000 adults living throughout the United Kingdom. Although this survey covered all aspects of people's lives as consumers, the problems and difficulties people encounter as pedestrians emerged as one of the most frequent single categories of complaint. It was this earlier survey that prompted us to undertake work specifically on pavements and the experiences of pedestrians (1).

The second survey was carried out for the present report by MORI (Market & Opinion Research International), as part of their regular fortnightly omnibus survey (2). This used a quota sample of 2,034 adults (aged 16 or over) living in Great Britain. Fieldwork was conducted in February 1986. Our questions covered:

★ the journeys people make on foot;
★ the main problems for pedestrians;
★ pedestrians' views on the safety and cleanliness of their environment;
★ pedestrian accidents and claims for compensation; and
★ whether a complaint had been made.

The Consumer Concerns study

Almost one in four of our respondents reported that they had encountered problems walking in the previous 12 months, and more than half of these problems were considered to be serious. The problems were highest among elderly people, and were higher among women than among men, but were nevertheless common to all ages and socio-economic groups.

The major cause of concern was the condition of pavements. Much of this concern was about broken or uneven surfaces, sometimes resulting from general neglect, but often caused by building work. A number of people had sustained quite serious injuries from trips and falls on damaged pavements, yet few of the sufferers had complained. Other problems included cars parking on pavements, fouling by dogs and pavement cycling (particularly by children). Some respondents were also concerned that local pavements were dangerously narrow or non-existent.

A shortage of pedestrian crossings was the second main source of concern. A number of respondents mentioned local petitions about the shortage of crossings, though these had usually been unsuccessful. Even when crossings existed, a few difficulties were reported, for instance with the lack of time allowed for crossing at pelican lights.

In general, the survey showed that the declining state of the environment was a major worry to a large number of people, and prompted

Table 2.1 Neighbourhood problems: regional breakdown

		Total	England	Wales	Scotland	Northern Ireland
Base:	weighted	**1,968**	1,633	98	187	50
	unweighted	**1,970**	1,198	247	277	248
		%	%	%	%	%
walking		**24**	25	18	26	7
dirty streets		**21**	21	21	19	17
public phone boxes*		**20**	21	12	24	8
street lighting		**19**	20	17	13	14
traffic or trains around home		**19**	20	14	12	9
road surfaces**		**(18)****	(19)**	(9)**	(24)**	(9)**
dust, smells, etc.		**14**	15	8	14	5
neighbours		**13**	14	11	9	4
rubbish collection		**12**	13	6	10	8
personally affected by vandalism and crime		**12**	13	7	15	11
wanted to complain		**11**	12	7	9	5

Notes
*Smaller sample size.
**Figures in brackets are based on total sample. When based on drivers the figures are: total 37%, England 36%, Wales 24%, Scotland 54%, Northern Ireland 19%.

Source: National Consumer Council, *An introduction to the findings of the consumer concerns survey*, NCC, August 1981.

us to suggest some 16 areas of consumers' lives where change could improve the quality of life for a significant number of people. Four were directly relevant to the present study:

★ cleaner, better-lit streets which present fewer difficulties to people walking;
★ less traffic in residential streets;
★ less pollution in residential areas;
★ better road surfaces.

A summary of pedestrian-related problems reported in the Consumer Concerns study is given in Table 2.1.

To a large extent it was the high level of pedestrian and neighbourhood concerns, relative to other areas of people's lives as consumers, that prompted our present work.

The MORI study

(a) Pedestrian problems

To find out what people are spontaneously worried about, we asked: 'What, if any, do you think are the main problems for pedestrians in your area?' Three problems stood out:

★ the volume of traffic (mentioned by 22 per cent of respondents);
★ cracked or uneven pavements (19 per cent);
★ lack of pedestrian crossings (11 per cent).

Only one in five failed spontaneously to identify any problems for pedestrians.

We then took respondents through a list of nineteen potential problems, asking them to identify which, if any, presented problems in their area.

Table 2.2 combines spontaneous and prompted answers, and ranks the problems according to how frequently they were reported. It also gives a breakdown by age, sex and socio-economic group.

In general, there were surprisingly few differences in the level of problems reported by people living in different types of area (urban, mixed or rural) although cracked/uneven pavements and pavement parking appear to be particular problems in urban areas, while people living in the country have more of a problem than city dwellers with narrow pavements. Respondents who had suffered a pedestrian accident in the previous year were more likely than the rest to mention cracked or uneven pavements (62 per cent); dog dirt (50 per cent); uncleared snow, ice or leaves (42 per cent); and uncleared litter (25 per cent). Similarly, people who had made a complaint were more likely than

Table 2.2 Main problems for pedestrians (prompted and unprompted)

Problem:	Total	Sex		Age					Socio-economic group			
		men	women	16–24	25–34	35–54	55–64	65+	AB	C1	C2	DE
Base (weighted)	2,034	967	1,067	403	358	599	285	389	349	453	629	603
	%	%	%	%	%	%	%	%	%	%	%	%
cracked or uneven pavements	46	39	52	38	44	43	53	54	40	44	46	51
dog dirt	42	39	44	32	43	40	45	50	42	40	41	43
too much traffic/busy roads	37	35	39	35	36	39	35	40	42	38	34	37
uncleared snow/ice/leaves	32	31	32	33	32	30	33	31	30	32	32	31
vehicles parked on pavements	24	21	26	20	24	22	26	27	16	26	25	25
no pedestrian crossing	23	23	23	25	26	24	17	20	22	24	22	24
bicycles ridden on pavements	19	19	20	15	17	17	21	29	17	18	19	23
litter/uncleared rubbish	17	17	17	12	13	19	21	21	18	19	15	18
pavements dug up/being repaired	13	12	14	13	14	13	14	13	15	12	11	16
poor/broken street lighting	13	12	13	16	15	13	10	8	12	10	15	12
narrow pavements	11	11	12	11	14	11	11	11	16	11	10	11
overhanging trees/hedges	11	9	13	8	8	12	16	14	15	10	10	12
too little time at pelicans	10	8	12	6	10	10	11	15	8	12	9	12
no pavements	7	8	6	6	7	9	7	5	10	6	7	6
weeds/overgrown hedges	6	6	6	5	4	6	7	9	8	6	5	6
no street lighting	6	6	6	8	9	6	6	2	5	5	7	7
kerbs too high	5	5	5	7	5	4	3	7	4	5	5	7
obstructions on pavements	4	5	4	4	3	5	5	5	4	5	4	6
need to use over/under passes	3	3	3	3	3	4	3	3	3	3	3	4
other	17	17	16	15	18	17	19	15	20	19	15	15
D/K	2	3	2	2	2	3	1	3	3	2	2	3
none—no problems	6	8	5	8	4	7	5	7	7	5	7	7

average to mention all the above problems and also vehicles parked on pavements (35 per cent); bicycles ridden on the pavement (34 per cent); and overhanging trees or hedges (18 per cent).

The problems (spontaneous and prompted combined) were also fairly evenly spread across people of different ages, socio-economic groups, regions, and sex. The following concerns stood out:

★ older people (aged 65 and over) were more likely than others to report problems with cracked/ uneven pavements (54 per cent); dog dirt (50 per cent) and bicycles ridden on pavements (29 per cent);

★ women tended to report more problems than men, but only just; they were, however, much more likely to report problems with cracked or uneven pavements (52 per cent, compared with 39 per cent for men);

★ people living in the south were more likely to report problems with vehicles parked on pavements (33 per cent).

We also looked at the relationship between the frequency with which people walk anywhere and the level of problems that they report. We divided respondents into four groups—those who walked to any particular destination (different sorts of shops, work, leisure, etc.) at least five days a week, those who walked to any particular destination at least once a week, those who ever walked anywhere and those who said they never made any journey entirely by foot. This last group reported fewer problems than the rest, but there were surprisingly few differences in the level of reported problems between the other three groups. However, differences began to emerge when we further divided the group of frequent walkers by the destinations to which they are walking. Respondents taking children to school or day-care facilities at least five days a week generally reported more problems than other people, as did people making frequent shopping trips—especially to main food shops but also to local food shops and shopping for other items.

Ten people in the survey were confined to wheelchairs. This number is much too small to allow us to report with confidence about their experiences, but it is worth pointing out that their problem level tended to be very high indeed, particularly with:

★ uncleared snow, ice or leaves (reported by about three-quarters of respondents)
★ litter/uncleared rubbish (three-quarters)
★ cracked pavements (three-quarters)
★ dog dirt (half)
★ too much traffic (half)
★ vehicles parked on pavements (a third)
★ cycles ridden on pavements (a third)

★ poor or broken-down street lights (a third)
★ high kerbs (a third).

(b) Views on pavement conditions

The survey suggests that almost half the adult population of Britain experience problems with cracked or uneven pavements in their neighbourhood. Even without prompting, nearly one in five people spontaneously mentioned cracked or uneven pavements as one of the main problems for pedestrians in their area.

Age, sex, class, and frequency of walking all appear to affect perceptions of this issue. Groups particularly likely to mention the condition of pavements as a problem were: women, people aged 55 and over, people from partly skilled or unskilled manual worker families and those on the lowest level of subsistence, and people who make frequent shopping trips on foot for food and other items, or who take children daily to school or day-care facilities.

In addition to the 46 per cent of respondents complaining of poorly-maintained pavement surfaces, 32 per cent reported problems with uncleared snow, ice or leaves (it should be noted that the survey was carried out in February 1986 during a period of exceptionally bad winter weather), and 13 per cent specifically reported problems with pavement excavations and repairs.

Other surveys and campaigns conducted independently by local groups point to the same conclusion: that the condition of our pavements is of serious concern to pedestrians and local residents. Some of these surveys highlight the special problems this presents to people with mobility handicaps. The Causey Campaign in Sheffield, for example, reported in 1985:

"By far the greatest number of problems (about using pavements) concerned hazardous paving stones and kerbstones. When the surface is uneven or broken the footing becomes unpredictable and pedestrians cannot rely on the ground they are about to tread on. Some people are able to watch the ground carefully and pick out the safest way forwards but by no means everybody is able to do this. Blind people have obvious problems but then, so do many others. For instance finding a safe, even way for the wheels on both sides of a pushchair or wheelchair is often quite impossible as it is when you are trying to place your feet, and your sticks or crutches safely on the ground." (3)

(c) Views on safety

Given the relatively high level of concern about some of the factors that affect pedestrian safety—such as the volume of traffic and the lack of pedestrian crossings—it is perhaps surprising that, when asked directly about safety, 84 per cent of the sample reported that conditions for pedestrians were safe.† This includes 18 per cent who described conditions as 'very safe' and 66 per cent who said they were 'fairly safe'. Roughly one in eight (12 per cent) said conditions were not very safe and 2 per cent not at all safe. A further 2 per cent gave no opinion.

Specific sub-groups more likely than others to say conditions for pedestrians were not very safe, or not at all safe included:

★ people who had complained about pavements, pedestrian areas or conditions for pedestrians in the previous 12 months (26 per cent);
★ people aged 65 and over (20 per cent);
★ people who had suffered any accident (including minor falls) as a pedestrian in the previous 12 months (19 per cent);
★ people with no car in the household (19 per cent, compared with 12 per cent of car owners);
★ people from social groups DE (unskilled manual workers) and those on the lowest level of subsistence (19 per cent);
★ women (18 per cent) rather than men (11 per cent).

It is notable that the presence of children in the household made little overall difference to people's views on safety, although respondents with children were less likely to say that conditions were *very* safe.

(d) Views on cleanliness

People were much more likely to criticise their neighbourhood on the grounds of cleanliness. The question we asked was: 'How clean would you say the pavements and pedestrian areas are around here? Would you say they are very clean, fairly clean, not very clean or not at all clean?'

Just over one-third (34 per cent) said that pavements and pedestrian areas in their neighbourhood were not clean (25 per cent 'not very clean' and nine per cent 'not at all clean'). One in ten respondents, on the other hand, described pavements and pedestrian areas as 'very clean' and 55 per cent as 'fairly clean'.

---

†The question was as follows: "How safe is it for you to get to the places you want to go to on foot? By safe, I mean in terms of traffic, roads and pavements. Would you say it is very safe, fairly safe, not very safe or not at all safe?"

There were no huge variations in the opinions of different groups. People more likely to say that pavements and pedestrian areas were unclean included:

★ people who had made a complaint about pedestrian matters in the previous 12 months (50 per cent said not very or not at all clean);
★ people who had had a fall or accident as a pedestrian (48 per cent);
★ frequent walkers, especially those walking at least five days a week to: schools/day-care facilities (46 per cent), for local food shopping (45 per cent) and non-food shopping (45 per cent);
★ people with children under five in the household (41 per cent);
★ people without cars (39 per cent);
★ old age pensioners (38 per cent); and
★ people from social groups DE—unskilled manual worker families and those living on the lowest level of subsistence (38 per cent).

Groups that were comparatively *unlikely* to describe their neighbourhoods as unclean included:

★ people living in rural areas (28 per cent found pavements and pedestrian areas not very or not at all clean);
★ people from social groups AB –professional and managerial workers families—(30 per cent);
★ people aged 16 to 24 (30 per cent);
★ full-time workers (30 per cent).

(e) Complaints

In the Consumer Concerns survey, people were more likely to have wanted to complain about their immediate neighbourhood than about anything else in their lives as consumers. In the subsequent MORI survey, we asked: 'In the past 12 months, have you made any complaints about pavements, pedestrian areas or conditions for pedestrians around here to anyone in authority?' Those who had made a complaint were then asked to whom they had complained.

Eighty-four per cent of respondents had made no complaint. Of the rest:

★ 5 per cent said they had complained to council staff;
★ 2 per cent to a local councillor;
★ 1 per cent to the police;
★ less than 0.5 per cent to a public service such as the gas or water boards; local/national press; or to their local MP;
★ 2 per cent to other people.

No one reported having complained to an advice centre.

Groups more likely to have made a complaint included people aged over 55 and people who said they never made any journey entirely by foot. Nearly half of this latter group were pensioners, and it is possible that their lack of mobility is caused, or at least exacerbated, by poor local provision for pedestrians.

The number of complaints made by the different groups did not necessarily coincide with their levels of reported problems. For example, people who had had accidents as pedestrians in the previous 12 months were not especially likely to have made a complaint. Indeed people who had suffered falls on slippery pavements were less likely to have made a complaint than those who had not had an accident. Similarly, fewer respondents with children under five in the household had made a complaint, even though they tended to report more problems.

Chapter 3 reports on pedestrian accidents—and on claiming compensation—in more detail.

NCC's postbag

In July 1985 the National Consumer Council issued a press release inviting consumer comment on their positive and negative experiences of being a pedestrian (see Appendix A).

The press release attracted wide coverage in national and regional newspapers, radio and TV reports. We logged a total of 536 letters in response, together with numerous photographs of cracked pavements and injuries caused, copies of correspondence between individuals and their local council, petitions from whole streets of people.

The size of our postbag is not, of course, a reliable or 'representative' guide to the scale of a particular problem, but it is perhaps worth recording that this was one of the largest public reactions we have ever had to a press release. It suggests the strength of feeling generated by pedestrian conditions.

While the letters mostly contained specific complaints about local conditions, two particular sources of dissatisfaction emerged: a perceived reluctance on the part of the police to enforce the laws on littering, dog-fouling, pavement-parking and cycling; and inaction by local councils in tackling poor pavement conditions. Many correspondents were elderly and perceived a general deterioration in pedestrian conditions over time. Some claimed that danger spots or areas of poor paving had remained unattended to for years. The letters revealed widespread cynicism about the willingness of the authorities to take action, even when specifically requested to do so.

"....for the last four years we have been complaining about the state of pavements on our local estate."

"For many months I have made representations to the local authority and police about heavy lorries parked on the footpath.... I also wrote to the local member of parliament, and local councillor."

"....we have been fighting for about 6 years.... I enclose only a few letters from the council/environmental /chief constable/deputy chief constable/local councillors/even our own MP... and still feel I am banging my head against a brick wall...."

We attempted to quantify the numerous different types of complaint mentioned. More than one in ten people (61 in all) referred to an accident sustained on broken or cracked pavements, and another dozen spoke of incidents involving cyclists. Most writers mentioned more than one problem, but, as Table 2.3 shows, the clear winners in the dissatisfaction league were broken pavements and dog dirt, consonant with the findings of our formal survey.

Table 2.3 NCC postbag of pedestrian concerns: most frequent mentions

Dog (and other animal) fouling	252
Badly maintained pavement	235
Pavement unrestored after digging up	54
Pavement broken by vehicles/parking	51
Pavement parking	183
Domestic litter (cans, chip papers etc)	178
Bicycles on pavements	132
Forced into road from hazards/obstructions on pavement	65
Ice/snow/leaves on pavement	63
Overhanging trees on pavement	48

Source: NCC correspondence, July–September 1985.

References to chapter 2

1. National Consumer Council, *An introduction to the findings of the consumer concerns survey*, NCC, August 1981.
2. Market & Opinion Research International, *Pedestrians*, summary report prepared for the National Consumer Council, MORI, February 1986.
3. John Mitchell, *The Causey Campaign, report by Working Party*, Sheffield Branch, National Federation (UK) of the Blind, July 1985.

Chapter 3
Accidents and compensation

Cracked, damaged, obstructed or badly maintained pavements are not merely a cause of annoyance—they are also a cause of accidents. Pedestrian accidents involving motor vehicles are recorded. Much less attention has been given to the more mundane but frequent range of accidents on the pavement such as slipping on ice or wet leaves; tripping on uneven paving stones, street furniture or rubbish; colliding with overhanging scaffolding or falling into unguarded holes caused by streetworks. We have attempted to investigate these 'hidden' accidents, and to look at the experiences of those victims who have tried to claim compensation.

Road accidents and pavement accidents

The definition of 'accident', under which official reporting is required and records kept, is:

> "One involving personal injury occurring on the public highway (including footways) in which a road vehicle is involved and which becomes known to the police within 30 days of its occurrence".(1)

The definition excludes from official records any pedestrian incident where no vehicle is involved. This category (mainly pavement accidents) is therefore effectively invisible to official view, though government mortality records show that in 1984 in England and Wales 189 people died in 'street and highway accidental falls' (2). A further seventeen such deaths were recorded in Scotland (3). Clearly, only a tiny proportion of pavement falls could be expected to prove fatal.

Although there is no systematic collection of information on pavement injuries, accident and emergency departments at hospitals readily acknowledge the frequency of these incidents. Medical studies have described injury-levels as being of 'epidemic' proportions, particularly during icy weather (4).

We have attempted to quantify the extent of the problem. In our two surveys—one by MORI, one by Consumers' Association—we asked, among other things, for information about pavement accidents over the previous twelve months (see Appendix A). Neither survey included children under sixteen years of age among whom trips and falls might be expected to be frequent. Both were carried out during periods which included some severe winter weather.

Roughly one in five of the MORI sample had reported an accident as a pedestrian in the previous year (including three per cent of the sample who had had more than one accident). Seven per cent had tripped or fallen on damaged pavements; eleven per cent had tripped or slipped on wet leaves, snow, ice or rubbish, and three per cent had walked into overhanging trees, scaffolding, obstructions and so on. A further one per cent mentioned accidents involving pedal cycles on pavements. The incidence of accidents reported by respondents in the CA sample was around one in ten.

The distribution of the main types of accident suffered was similar in the two surveys. Just over half of accidents in both samples involved tripping and slipping on wet leaves, snow, etc; and over one-third (36 per cent in both groups) concerned tripping and falling on damaged pavements. A small proportion of the respondents in the MORI survey had been injured by pavement obstructions such as overhanging trees (15 per cent of accident victims).

Table 3.1 Details of injury and damage in pavement accidents, MORI survey

	Total	Tripped/ fell on damaged pavement	Tripped on wet leaves, snow, etc.	Walked into obstruction
	%	%	%	%
Medical treatment				
treated at hospital	**5**	6	2	—
treated by GP	**2**	3	1	—
no treatment needed	**93**	91	97	100
Damage				
damage to clothes/belongings	**17**	24	12	6
no damage to clothes/belongings	**83**	76	88	94
unweighted bases	**(400)**	(144)	(218)	(63)

Source: Market & Opinion Research International, *Pedestrians, a summary report for NCC*, page 16, MORI, February 1986.

As Table 3.1 shows, nearly one in ten of the people in the MORI survey who had tripped or fallen on damaged pavements needed some medical treatment, and almost a quarter incurred damage to clothes or belongings. A slightly higher proportion of respondents in the CA sample recorded injuries or damage.

Clearly, pavement accidents are an everyday occurrence. In the absence of any official national statistics, a very tentative idea of the extent and seriousness of such accidents can be gained by applying the results of the MORI survey to the total UK population. The calculation is based on an adult (16 years and over) population of Britain of 41 million.

Table 3.2 Calculation of accidents, adult UK population

Accident in the past 12 months	6.5 to 8.5 million
(a) trips and falls on damaged pavements	2.3 to 3.4 million
(b) trips and slips on wet leaves/ice and snow/rubbish	4 to 5 million
(Calculated within 95% confidence limits.)	

Pavement accidents are far more common than pedestrian accidents involving motor vehicles. Unsurprisingly, pavement accident victims are far less likely to require medical treatment than pedestrian victims of accidents involving a vehicle. From the CA sample, the percentages of accident victims needing different types of treatment can be calculated. Over half of all pedestrian victims of motor accidents needed some form of treatment.

Table 3.3 Treatment needed by accident victims (as percentage)

	In-patient	Out-patient	GP
trip/slip	1.1	9.4	6.8
motor vehicle	20.3	25.0	18.8

Notes

*The figures for pavement accidents have been derived by adding two categories: 'tripped on damaged pavement' and 'slipped on wet leaves, snow, ice, etc.'

*There may be some multi-coding reflected in these figures—for example the same accident might require both in-patient and out-patient treatment. As far as we can tell, the effect is to reduce the absolute number of cases by less than 10%. We have no reason to believe that the *relative* position of pavement accidents and vehicle accidents would be changed by recoding.

However, pavement accident victims outnumber vehicle accident victims by such a large amount that, in absolute terms, the numbers needing medical treatment are far greater:

Table 3.4 Treatment needed by accident victims (numbers of cases from CA survey)

	In-patient	Out-patient	GP
trip/slip	30	247	178
motor vehicle	13	16	12

Please see notes to Table 3.3.

Of the total number of people in the survey who had needed medical treatment in the previous year (as the result of either a pavement fall or an accident involving a motor vehicle) over 90 per cent were the result of falls, only eight per cent were accounted for by a vehicle accident.

Again, in the absence of any more precise official statistics on the numbers of pavement accident victims needing medical treatment, our surveys allow crude calculations to be carried out, though with less confidence than can be attached to the overall estimates of accident rates. Based again on an adult UK population of 41 million, the MORI survey suggests that about 450,000 injuries requiring medical treatment are sustained each year as a result of pavement falls. The CA survey suggests a slightly larger figure (about 600,000 per year on a conservative estimate) though it must be emphasised that this survey was not based on a random sample of the whole UK population.

The very fact that these calculations need to be made is itself significant as it points up a contrast in the recording of different sorts of accident. In the case of accidents sustained in the home, a detailed surveillance system has been set up by the Department of Trade and Industry (5). This fairly recent development is itself still relatively modest compared with the recording of accidents at work. It is, however, a most welcome development, and one that confronts some of the same methodological challenges that the recording of pavement accidents would pose.

According to the report of the 1984 data '...the overall number of home accidents annually in Great Britain that require some form of medical treatment is of the order of 3 million' (6). However, it should be noted that about 43 per cent of home accidents recorded in DTI's own statistics involved children under 16. The overall number of home accidents involving adults might therefore be estimated at about 1,750,000. While this is clearly greater than the number of pavement fall accidents suggested by our surveys, we would suggest that the difference is not so great as to justify the disparity in the seriousness with which they are apparently viewed officially. Indeed the DTI has carried out detailed investigations into types of accidents involving only a few thousand victims a year, for example a report on skateboard accidents (7).

The seriousness of a proportion of pavement accidents is really quite dramatic. We sought more detailed information from people who had written to the NCC or the Pedestrians' Association about their accidents, by sending a self-completion questionnaire to approximately 100 accident victims. We received 75 valid returns. This provided some case histories that demonstrate the types of injuries that can be sustained in pavement accidents.

The majority of accidents in the case histories (56) involved pavement trips; four were a result of cycle-riders, and three a combination of slipping and tripping, sometimes involving public utility streetworks. Respondents were overwhelmingly middle-aged to elderly. Nearly two-thirds received hospital treatment of some kind. There were 42 cases of broken bones, including 11 wrist fractures, eight arm/elbow fractures, one person with a broken collar bone and another with fractured spinal vertabrae. Other injuries included 26 cases mentioning bruising and swelling, cuts and grazes (11), damage to teeth (3), permanent loss of an eye, two cases of concussion, and four people suffering from strain, stress or shock.

One person was in hospital for five weeks and subsequently house-bound for two years:

"I have been registered disabled 1.11.85. Cannot walk properly. I was such an active person all my life."

Another correspondent commented that:

'... the 12 people at physiotherapy last Autumn (including myself) were all victims of the pavements.'

Our sample of accident victims also revealed other losses: 48 people mentioned damage to clothes, glasses and other belongings. Twenty-two people had to take time off work as a result of the accident, varying from one week to seven months' absence. Someone lost their part-time job, another person gave up their voluntary work. Two people of retirement age had to give up their casual work.

Whose fault?

Some commentators reject the use of the term 'accident' at all.

"According to the Oxford English Dictionary, the two principal ingredients of an accident are that it is an *unexpected event* and that its occurrence is attributed to chance... We would argue that the term 'accident' is highly value-laden: it implies a sense of inevitability (bad luck, act of God), which is counterproductive to any attempt by society to prevent the occurrence of accidents." (8)

There is, of course an element of chance in most accidents, and the behaviour of victims themselves might also contribute to the probability of an accident occurring; for example, drunken pedestrians are more likely to be involved in a road accident. We might expect a sense of fatalism to be particularly widely applied to pavement accidents, which are frequently undramatic in their effects—sixty per cent of pavement fall victims in the MORI survey considered their accident 'not serious enough' to warrant a claim for compensation.

However, it appears from our surveys that only a small minority of pavement accident victims believe that they are to blame. In the MORI sample, four people of the 132 who had fallen on uneven pavements said they thought it was their own fault. Ten (six per cent) of those slipping on ice/snow or rubbish blamed themselves. In the CA sample, 290 people—nearly a fifth of those who had slipped—said the accident was their own fault. Again, pavement trip victims were less likely to blame themselves (105 out of 1,007, a little over ten per cent).

We asked our panel of 75 accident victims directly whose fault they thought the accident was. No one considered it was his or her own fault. A majority blamed the accident on pavement conditions and, by extension, the highway authority.

"The pavement needs resurfacing. It is not fit to walk on. Even my grandchild has tripped and fallen..."

"This was not my first fall as the pavements in Ayr are a disgrace."

"All town centre pavements are uneven. Two friends have fallen in the same way.... The quality of workmanship is abysmal..."

"The pavements in the centre of Salisbury are generally in poor condition, particularly that paving slabs are cracked, broken or dislodged. My daughter suffered a similar accident about 20 years ago, which illustrates the Council's lack of attention..."

The present law

The English legal system of compensation is based on proving fault. One of the inadequacies of such a system is clear in the case of victims of hit-and-run accidents. Because the driver cannot be traced, many victims assume that they can get no compensation as they can find no one to blame. This is especially serious for pedestrians who account for one-third of such victims (9).

In fact there is a special statutory scheme run by the Motor Insurers' Bureau, which is legally liable to pay damages to the victims of hit-and-run accidents and to those injured by uninsured drivers. However, evidence shows that this scheme is little known, and therefore under-used. Perhaps two-thirds of such victims fail to find out about it (10).

We feel that the availability of compensation from this source should be more widely advertised, and those who come into contact with victims, for example police officers and hospital staff, should be made aware of its existence.

A further disincentive to seeking compensation under the law's tort system is 'contributory negligence', where the victim may be held partly to blame for the accident and his or her compensation reduced accordingly.

To succeed at law in obtaining compensation for a pavement accident a pedestrian must first prove that the pavement was dangerous to pedestrians; secondly that there was a failure to repair that danger; thirdly that as a result of failing to repair that danger, damage was caused to the pedestrian. Even if the victim establishes these facts, his or her claim may fail if the local authority proves that it had taken such care as in all the circumstances was reasonably required to ensure that the pavement was not dangerous to pedestrians.

There is no duty on a highway authority immediately to repair a defective pavement. However, once they are aware of the danger they must act promptly. Pavement victims will usually succeed against the authority if it can be shown that someone had earlier complained about the danger of that particular stretch of pavement. It is therefore important that people complain about dangerous pavements, to help others who might fall on the same defect if it remains unrepaired.

In icy conditions, the duty to maintain the pavement by removing snow and ice so that it is safe for pedestrians remains. However, whether there has been a breach of that duty is a question of fact and degree. The courts will look at the nature and importance of the pavement and the time that elapsed before the snow and ice was cleared or gritted. In 1978 the Court of Appeal decided that it was reasonable for highway authorities to have a priority of clearing major roads before pavements. In that case Lord Denning said: 'I should have thought everyone knew that, if he walked out on a road or footpath made slippery or dangerous with ice or snow, he did so at his own risk'. This is an extreme, if not personal, statement of the law and pedestrians have recovered damages for accidents that have occurred on icy pavements. However, it is clear that the courts expect pedestrians to take greater care of themselves when the weather conditions are bad and therefore a finding of contributory negligence is more likely.

Claiming damages

For road accident victims, redress can only really be gained by seeking compensation from the other party, which involves proving fault. About one in three of all known road accident victims do so, but not all the claims succeed. A major review of personal injury compensation, conducted by the Oxford Socio-Legal Studies Group in the late 1970s, found that 29 per cent of those involved in road accidents received some damages (11). A Research Institute for Consumer Affairs study, of two sets of pedestrian and cyclist victims of road accidents, found that 86 out of 324 had made some attempt to claim compensation, representing 27 per cent of the total (12).

The National Consumer Council's samples showed similarly low levels of claims. In our MORI survey, only four claims had been made by 21 car-accident victims, although seven had required medical treatment and six sustained damage to belongings. Two compensation claims were still unresolved, one had been unsuccessful, and one successful. None of the four victims of motorcycle accidents had claimed compensation. In the much larger CA sample, twelve out of 57 car-accident victims had lodged compensation claims, and three of the 40 motorcycle victims. All the motorcycle claims were unresolved, along with half of the car claims. Of the remaining six car claims, half had received compensation, the other half had not.

In three instances of car accidents, CA respondents did *not* make a claim because, 'the identity of the third party was unknown'. These respondents may well have been able to claim from the Motor Insurers' Bureau scheme.

In general, studies on personal injury and tort compensation have shown that there is very little relationship between either the severity of injury or blameworthiness and the likelihood of obtaining compensation. Although road accident victims are among the groups most likely to claim, the proportion who do so is still low, and dependent largely upon someone advising individuals of their rights. Claims often take a long time to complete, with delays being caused both by insurance companies and by the legal process.

Pavement-accident victims are even less likely to claim compensation than those involved in road accidents: 87 per cent in the MORI survey failed to claim, and 97 per cent of the CA sample. The main reasons given by people in the MORI survey for not claiming are shown in Table 3.5. (The CA survey results followed these closely, with the exception that respondents were more likely to blame themselves for the accident.) Some six out of every ten accidents were thought 'not serious enough' to warrant a claim. Lack of awareness of legal rights and worries about the effort involved in making a claim were also significant factors.

Table 3.5 Reasons for not claiming compensation

	Tripped/fell on damaged pavement	Slipped wet leaves/ ice/snow etc	Walked into obstruction
Bases	(135)	(181)	(56)
	%	%	%
Accident not serious enough	59	60	47
Didn't know could claim	13	10	7
Too much effort/trouble to make claim	12	4	6
Accident was own fault	3	6	5
Other	4	3	5
Don't know/can't remember	11	19	30

Source: Market & Opinion Research International, *Pedestrians*, page 16, MORI, February 1986.

Only one person in the MORI sample had claimed for tripping on a pavement, without success, and one other was awaiting the outcome of a claim for a slipping-up accident. The CA group revealed 26 successful claims for trips, slips and obstruction accidents, another 13 unsuccessful, and 18 cases pending, from a total of 2,742 incidents.

Our panel of 75 accident victims revealed a much higher claim rate: 32 people against 37 not claiming. The group was self-selecting in that they had previously contacted either the Pedestrians' Association for advice on claiming, or NCC to inform us of their accident. It is reasonable to assume that their motivation for seeking redress was higher than average, a conclusion borne out by the finding that 34 members of this group also sought advice over the accident, in 19 cases from more than one source.

We asked 'who did you seek advice from?':

citizens advice bureau	13
another advice centre	2
solicitor	19
council/councillor	11
police	2
friend/neighbour	5
Pedestrians' Association	11
other	5

There were 13 successful claims, 14 were refused compensation and seven cases were outstanding at the time of questionnaire completion.

From our own surveys, local sources and the sparse national information available, it is possible to build up a tentative description of the reasons why so few compensation claims are made.

(a) Ignorance of right to claim

About 10 per cent of MORI respondents who had suffered an accident as a pedestrian gave this as a reason for not claiming compensation. Little attempt is made to publicise this right.

As mentioned above, an avenue of claim about which very few people seem to be aware is the Motor Insurers' Bureau. Although the main group of pedestrians likely to want to claim under this scheme are victims of hit-and-run road accidents, we understand that the Motor Insurers' Bureau could also make awards in cases of pavement trips, where it was established that a vehicle had been responsible for cracking the pavement. This, of course, is very difficult to substantiate in most cases. The Motor Insurers' Bureau would also consider claims from slips on oily patches, or trips over car debris left in the path of the victim. However, the Motor Insurers' Bureau itself does not publicise this information, nor even keep a record of how many claims of this kind it deals with.

(b) Confusion over responsibility, and proving fault

There is a complex system of responsibilities for pavement maintenance. Seven of our accident-victim claimants sought payment from utility or other companies who had dug up the pavements. A couple of cases involved shop or public house frontages. One woman eventually received £1,400 from a personal accident injury policy after abandoning her compensation claim:

"I was in a no-win situation. To proceed through the courts would have been costly, as first I had to establish the legal ownership of the hole in the pavement... Both Council and shop/property owners disclaimed ownership."

On a brighter note, one respondent found unexpected assistance:

"It was *not* my initial intent to claim for compensation, but this matter was referred to the Kent County Council who took this up with the SE Gas Board."

This woman eventually received £800 in compensation.

An informal agreement between Municipal Mutual (the main local authority insurers) and some public utilities governs temporary pavement surfaces; up to 12 months the utility is responsible, between 12 to 24 months liability is split between utility and council, and thereafter the council is responsible. This arrangement is, however, neither binding nor publicised.

(c) 'Not worth the effort'

A further group are deterred from lodging or pursuing a claim by their fear of becoming entangled in a complex, and perhaps expensive, legal process. The chances of winning significant compensation seem to be lowly rated.

> "It seemed a waste of time after reading about more serious cases than mine and the treatment they had received from councils."

> "Regret not getting legal advice. But thought it might be expensive to get solicitor and have to pay money to fight for compensation as they say you can't win when you're dealing with (the council)."

(d) Discouragement from claiming

Sometimes, this impression seems to be reinforced by the local authorities themselves.

> "Council were off hand on phone and said I had to prove it was their fault."

> "Council wrote and said the pavement wasn't 1/2" sticking up. I found the letter from the council very uncaring, and more or less said I should look where I was going..."

Some had declined to pursue a case on advice from independent sources. Five of our accident victims were advised they had no grounds to claim. Others were warned of the likely expense, poor chances of legal aid, uncertainty of the outcome. A couple of people claim to have been 'warned off' by the local authority.

> "CAB suggested a 'free' solicitor who would give 30 mins advice free—but did not take this up—council in correspondence warned me I would get nothing if I went to solicitor."

> "(The County Council) wrote to me saying I would lose my teacher's salary if I claimed (for the period absent)."

These negative experiences contrast somewhat with the procedures outlined by some councils for complaints-handling on footway trips (13). Several indicated that they would send a claim form to the complainant, and in some cases a highway inspector would visit as well. Reading and Southampton councils both said that they would forward claims to other authorities where relevant, and inform the claimant that they had done so.

Despite these efforts by at least some councils, public confidence over claims-handling still seems to be low, and it may be that the formal procedures adopted by councils are not always uniformly applied in the handling of individual cases.

It appears to be common practice for local authorities or insurance companies to argue that obstructions of less than three-quarters of an inch (or 20 millimetres) do not legally constitute a danger, and therefore to disclaim liability. The real position seems to be more complicated.

Under section 58 of the Highways Act 1980, the highway authority can put up a defence against claims for damage if it can prove that it has taken 'reasonable care' to make sure that the pavement in question was not dangerous. The section says nothing about how big an obstruction must be before it is considered dangerous: in fact it suggests a number of factors that should be taken into account, including the 'character of the highway' and the 'state of repair in which a reasonable person would expect to find the highway'.

The standard of care that the courts expect of the local authorities in maintaining their pavements is not a high one. It has been said several times that a highway is not to be criticised by the standards of a bowling green. There is, however, no common test to establish whether a given paving stone was dangerous. A number of cases have suggested that a projecting edge of 20mm (or three-quarters of an inch) is to be used as a rule-of-thumb minimum for a paving stone to be in need of repair, but courts must look at the nature and importance of the pavement: a broken or uneven paving stone outside an old people's home could be a danger while an identically defective paving stone in a cul-de-sac might not be.

In January 1980 the Court of Appeal heard a case (*Lawman v. Waltham Forest*) involving this precise question. Lord Justice Stephenson, in his summing up, said:

"In my view, the citation of cases of tripping needs to be carefully controlled. I am not prepared to adopt the view that because in some cases trips of three-quarters of an inch, one inch, or half an inch were held to be or not to be a danger, that is a finding which has any binding force upon this or any other court."

Lord Justice Stephenson further quoted—apparently approvingly—Edmond-Davies' statement that there is no '... blanket rule that trips of three quarters of an inch or less cannot amount to a danger.' The conclusion seems to be that the question of whether a pavement fault is dangerous or not can only be decided by the particular circumstances of the case—the fact that it was lower than 20 millimetres proves nothing on its own.

In view of this, some examples of official correspondence to consumers that we have seen are positively misleading.

Example 1
"You may not be aware of a High Court decision which states that trips of up to 1″ are not to be considered dangerous in normal circumstances."
(Insurance company denial of liability)

Example 2
"The courts do not award damages where the trip is under one inch and consequently I must deny liability for the fall."
(Local authority letter to claimant)

Example 3
"Courts have found that trips less than 25mm do not impose liability upon the body who own the particular piece of street apparatus. I regret therefore that I cannot recommend any payment to you in respect of your claim."
(Public utility insurance office letter to claimant)

Example 1 is a carefully worded and technically accurate explanation, which leaves much unsaid. Its effect could be to mislead. Examples 2 and 3 are both inaccurate and misleading.

Compare the blanket denial of liability in Example 2 above with the assurance given to a member of the Pedestrians' Association seeking information on claims-handling by a major insurance company:

"It is however, necessary, I feel, to assure you that each and every claim received is considered on its own merits and although measurements may be a factor in determining liability, it would certainly not be the only one."

The evidence we have seen suggests that the actual behaviour of authorities and insurance companies falls far short of these standards, and is often intended to have the effect of stopping legitimate claims from proceeding.

(e) Delay in settlement

Municipal Mutual insurance company estimated that 50 per cent of highway claims handled by them are settled within a year of notification by councils, and 90 per cent between thirteen and twenty-four months after notification, which is about average for all personal injury settlements according to the Oxford study (14). Most councils, they say, provide details within two weeks of an accident, but it is not unknown for a council to take six months to produce a report (15).

This is borne out by the four available Ombudsman cases: three in England and one in Wales, where maladministration was found against councils for delays in dealing with claims for footway falls. Delay is a feature of all personal injury cases, and a factor both in reducing the eventual sum agreed and the numbers of people continuing the claim, a point not lost on one claimant still awaiting settlement: 'The length of time taken appears to be unnecessarily long and in my view may be deliberate in the hope that I will give up. I won't.'

Twelve settlements among our accident victims ranged from one month to eighteen months, with an average of seven and a half months. In the four outstanding cases, two had been going for about a year, and the others for 18 months and nearly three and a half years respectively.

The crucial point about compensation settlements is that, with the exception of the small minority of cases which end up in court, the outcome is the result of a bargaining process, and reflects the relative knowledge, skills and nerve of the parties involved. For the aggrieved party every new stage involves a gamble: whether the additional legal costs of holding out will cancel the possible increase in award, whether a defence of contributory negligence will succeed, whether they can afford to keep going for another few weeks or months without the cash in hand.

The costs of accidents and the value of settlements

The Department of Transport makes official estimates of the cost of road accidents, based on criteria of loss of economic output from death or injury; ambulance and hospital treatment; pain, suffering and grief to victim/relatives; damage to vehicles and property; police and insurance administration costs. The figures are issued annually, and it is stressed in the official note (16) that they are to be regarded as *minima*, particularly because elements such as pain and suffering are very hard to put a cash value to. Yet the estimates are considered important because: 'the amount and distribution of expenditure on road safety depends, to some extent, on the value of savings in accident costs estimated to follow such expenditure' (17).

On these estimates, at 1984 prices, road accidents for that year cost *£2,650 million* in total. Each person killed was estimated to cost £161,170 to society, with figures of £7,520 for serious casualties and £190 per slight casualty. The average cost of pedestrian casualties, at £6,960 per victim, was the highest average of any single class of road user, reflecting the higher proportion of serious and fatal injuries to pedestrians.

The extent of *personal* costs suffered by the individual and/or their families arising from accidents is not systematically valued or recorded. In a handful of particularly serious cases of personal injury, courts will make compensation assessments running into hundreds of thousands of pounds.

The Research Institute for Consumer Affairs (RICA) conducted a study in 1980 into the personal and financial consequences for pedestrian and cyclist victims of road accidents (18). As well as the 'cash' costs incurred the study draws attention to the multiplicity of other, less quantifiable, side-effects such as loss of earnings, loss of ability to work, absence from full-time education, unpaid care by relatives and their consequential loss of earnings in some cases, local authority care, disruption to households caused by severe or permanent incapacity or death. Although no similar study has been conducted in respect of pavement accident victims, the consequences will clearly be similar.

The RICA road accident victims survey found that only 26 out of 49 families who had received compensation believed the amount covered their financial loss from the accident. The survey describes awards as 'relatively modest'. Further, it was seen that the amount of compensation relative to financial loss varied widely: 'In most cases compensation was between a quarter and 15 times the reported loss. In two cases it was apparently around 50 times, and in a further two cases around 100 times.'(19)

RICA concluded that the tort compensation system works poorly for road accident victims. They commended the proposals of the Pearson Commission for a 'no-fault' compensation scheme to be available for all injured people involved in road accidents, paid for from a levy on petrol as part of the social security system of benefits. Such a scheme would operate in addition to tort compensation. RICA does point out, however, that Pearson's proposals would not cover accidents where no motor vehicle was involved. A 'no-fault' scheme is also recommended by the Pedestrians' Association, and was in June 1986 the subject of a House of Commons ten-minute-rule Bill introduced by Greville Janner QC MP.

In pavement accidents, settlements are likely to be even less common. Most local authorities are insured to meet these types of claims. However, there is very little information publicly available from either the councils themselves or the insurance companies on the extent of claims or levels of settlements. In NCC's questionnaire survey of selected district councils, we sought some fairly detailed information about footway trips and falls, and compensation claims. Six of the nineteen councils replying could provide no information at all on claims. In the other cases, 1984/85 numbers of claims ranged from 13 in Wycombe, to 300 in Middlesbrough, with an average of 78 per authority. The average for 1985/86 was higher, at 90, although four councils showed slight decreases.

The lack of claims information was commented on in the *Report on Footway Maintenance 1979-80* (20) when rough figures were given suggesting an average cost of claim settlement amounted to two to four per cent of the annual footway maintenance budget.

A more recent estimate is given in the 1983 publication, *Local Authorities' Highway Maintenance Code of Practice*, where it is suggested that highway claims cost £7 million a year (21). Unfortunately no breakdown is given of the proportion of this total which relates to *footway* claims, although Municipal Mutual insurance company (who handle most councils' insurance, and from whose survey the above figure was arrived at) has told us that 95 per cent of highway claims relate to pedestrian accidents. What is reasonably clear is that the numbers of claims are increasing and also, according to Municipal Mutual, the proportion which are met. They estimated that 60-66 per cent of the 80,000 highway claims processed by them annually are now met, as against 45-50 per cent in 1979-80.

The explanation given for this is a deterioration in footway conditions, making it harder for councils to repudiate claims.

"Obviously maintenance standards do have a bearing on the number of claims, and the growing cost of awards in the courts must improve the economic case for more expenditure designed to prevent claims." (22)

Despite this growth, we believe the figures still represent a very small proportion of *potential* claims. Municipal Mutual also acknowledge that the level of settlement varies enormously between areas. The figure given for average settlements in the now-abolished metropolitan counties was £500-£1,000. Only Southampton (which does not have an outside insurer) and Elmbridge were able to supply full information for NCC's questions on claims settlements. Southampton's average payment in

1984/85 was £71, and in 1985/86, £103. Elmbridge recorded an average of £116 in 1984/85, and £83 in 1985/86.

Among the panel of accident victim respondents, the thirteen cases of successful claims produced an average of £591. However, apart from two instances (£2,500 and £1,013.75) the rest were below £1,000, and eight were £500 or less. Three people settled for under £100.

Those claims relating to public utilities or other 'third parties' are of course not handled by councils at all, and would not be included in any of the above estimates. The *Report on Footway Maintenance* stated that anything up to half of claims initially received by councils came into this category, but no further information on the progress of these claims is available.

Municipal Mutual insurance company accepted the inequalities of the bargaining process where pedestrians are involved in pressing compensation claims. Their own policy in handling 'serious' (ie. large) claims is to insist that they are dealt with through a solicitor, clearly to protect themselves as well as the claimant. Only a very small number of cases, maybe 500 per year, will go to court. The remainder are settled either through an ex gratia payment (where the company considers the case borderline) or an offer of compensation.

Four of the 19 councils providing claims information to NCC indicated that they would make ex gratia payments themselves in some instances. One council, which does not have an outside insurer, explained that

> "For minimal claim e.g. torn tights arising out of a trip over a minor defect, we may pay ex gratia claim as it is cheaper than arguing liability."

Another told us of having authority from its insurers

> "to settle claims up to £100 where no injury is involved, i.e. damaged clothing etc. and in genuine cases these are normally settled promptly without argument."

A third council would pay if the claim was low, the circumstances proved that the council was liable, the accident involved only damage to property, not injury to the claimant and public relations would be improved. The fourth council simply stated 'Without prejudice for damage to clothing only—Never when personal injury has occurred.'

It is possible that, were more local authorities to adopt similar approaches to damage-only "out of pocket expenses" for footway trips, this could provide a quick and simple form of redress for a substantial number of victims at minimal cost to the councils, and with major benefits in retaining public good will in terms of the perceived justice of the outcome.

References to chapter 3

1. Department of Transport, *Road accidents Great Britain 1984*, p.4, HMSO, November 1985.
2. Office of Population Censuses and Surveys, *1984 mortality statistics, accidents and violence*, series DH4, No.10, Table 4, HMSO, 1986.
3. Information supplied by General Registrar's Office, Edinburgh.
4. See, for example, Merrild and Bak, 'An excess of pedestrian injuries in icy conditions: a high-risk fracture group—elderly women', *Accident Analysis and Prevention*, Vol.15, No.1, pp.41-48, 1983. Z.A. Ralis, 'Epidemic of fractures during period of snow and ice', *British Medical Journal*, Vol.282, 21 February 1981.
5. Department of Prices and Consumer Protection, *The home accident surveillance system*, a report of the first six months' data collection, DPCP, 1977.
6. Department of Trade and Industry, *The home accident surveillance system*, report of 1984 data, p.3, DTI, 1985.
7. Department of Prices and Consumer Protection, *The home accident surveillance system*, analysis of skateboard accidents, DPCP, 1979.
8. A.J. Chapman, F.M. Wade and H.C. Foot (eds), *Pedestrian accidents*, ch.1, pp.1-2, John Wiley and Sons Ltd, 1982.
9. Department of Transport, *Road accidents Great Britain 1985*, HMSO, November 1986.
10. The survey by the Research Institute for Consumer Affairs of road accident victims' compensation claims found that of seventeen hit-and-run incidents, five victims later claimed from the MIB, whilst eleven more had not been told of the existence of the scheme (the twelfth victim was uncontactable). Research Institute for Consumer Affairs, *Knocked down: a study of the personal and family consequences of road accidents involving pedestrians and pedal cyclists*, Consumers' Association, February 1980.
11. D. Harris et al., *Compensation and support for illness and injury*, Oxford Socio-Legal Studies, Clarendon Press, 1984.
12. Research Institute for Consumer Affairs, *op.cit.*, pp.22, 24.
13. National Consumer Council questionnaire survey of selected district councils, The pedestrian environment, June 1986.
14. D. Harris et al., *op.cit.*
15. Municipal Mutual insurance company representative in discussion with NCC, June 1986.
16. Department of Transport, *Highways Economics Note No. 1 Road accident costs 1984*, DTp, September 1985.
17. Department of Transport, *Road accidents Great Britain 1984*, p.31, HMSO, November 1985.

18. Research Institute for Consumer Affairs, *op.cit.*

19. Research Institute for Consumer Affairs, *op.cit.*, pp.32-33.

20. Standing Committee on Highway Maintenance, *A study of footway maintenance 1979-80*, p.14, December 1981.

21. Association of County Councils, Association of District Councils, Association of Metropolitan Authorities, *Highway maintenance: a code of good practice*, ACC, ADC, AMA, July 1983.

22. *Ibid*, p.18.

Chapter 4
Pavements: what goes wrong?

We have seen that nearly half the adult population of Great Britain may experience problems with cracked or uneven pavements in their neighbourhood. Out of all the consumer surveys we have conducted at the National Consumer Council, this is one of the highest problem levels we have ever recorded. In this chapter we look in more detail at the question of damaged pavements, attempt to spotlight some of the weaknesses in current arrangements for maintaining roads and pavements, and suggest ways these might be tackled.

Evidence of physical conditions

Since 1976, a physical survey, called the National Road and Maintenance Conditions Survey (NRMCS), has been carried out each year on 100-metre stretches of randomly-selected highways for the Department of Transport's Standing Committee on Highway Maintenance. The survey includes virtually all highway authorities in England and Wales, with Scotland organising its own similar survey. Survey criteria and standards are issued from the Standing Committee, and the actual inspection work is done by local authority highway inspectors themselves.

Data on pavement defects has been collected since the survey began, but has only recently been published as part of the survey. They are categorised in two ways:

★ footway deterioration: the proportion of the footway area with a badly disintegrated or deformed surface, likelihood of standing water, cracked or uneven paving flags or badly weed-ridden surface;

★ footway trips: the number of spot conditions constituting a specific danger to pedestrians.

The report for 1985 concludes that although carriageway conditions have deteriorated since 1980—and are now in a worse condition than they were in 1977—there has been no marked change in footway conditions over the period 1977-1985. While it remained at a constant level, the extent of deterioration seems high: the NRMCS records a general footway deterioration level of 20 per cent, and a trip rate of one in every 40 metres of footway. Urban roads—especially unclassified roads—have a higher number of trips per 100 metres (two to three) than trunk or rural roads (one), while footway deterioration is highest on principal roads in rural areas (29 per cent in 1985) (1).

The survey itself has one technical problem as far as footway conditions are concerned. Unlike defects in the carriageway, those in the footway are not precisely defined. For example, no measurement is given to define an uneven paving flag, and the notes for inspectors further suggest that 'judgement must to some extent be related to footway usage, a more critical assessment being made on heavily used surfaces.' The report's evaluation of footway conditions may therefore be less reliable than relating to carriageways, and the trend should be treated with caution.

Causes of footway deterioration

According to a special study of footway maintenance carried out for the Standing Committee on Highway Maintenance in 1979-80 (2), natural deterioration is the primary cause of footway defects. However, two other factors were also identified as being significant: over-riding by vehicles, especially heavy lorries, and public utility operations. These latter causes of damage have nothing to do with the use of pavements by pedestrians, who are in fact doubly disadvantaged: through losing the use of the pavement while it is dug up or parked on, and then through the long-term effects of the cracked and damaged paving stones.

Looking at conditions, procedures and practices in four areas the study team found that for planned maintenance work (that is, an annual programme planned in advance), the main causes of the defects were as follows:

natural deterioration	87 per cent
over-riding by vehicles	54 per cent
public utility operations	26 per cent

As can be seen from these percentages, for much of the work no single cause could be isolated. For basic maintenance jobs on the other hand, the following causes were specified:

natural deterioration	54 per cent
over-riding	28 per cent
public utility operations	12 per cent
other	6 per cent

Other causes might include poor workmanship; inferior materials; heavy objects dropped on to the footway; loose, projecting or sunken stopcock covers and manhole surrounds; and damage by tree roots and weeds.

Tackling the problems

What is the purpose of footway maintenance, from the consumer's point of view?

The Code of Practice on highway maintenance, prepared by the local authority associations, defines the object of footway maintenance as being 'to provide a reasonably safe path for pedestrians by day and by night' (3). The report on footway maintenance from the Standing Committee on Highway Maintenance goes further by stating that 'the primary objective of footway maintenance is to keep footways safe and comfortable for pedestrians, with some regard for appearance, while ensuring that expenditure is both cost-effective and justified in terms of present and likely future use' (4).

We support this last objective, although we would like explicit recognition of the fact that pavements should be safe and comfortable for all pedestrians who might reasonably want to use them. This means ensuring that conditions are satisfactory for the most vulnerable users— the elderly, young children, and people with mobility handicaps.

The duty to maintain

Highway authorities have a clear duty to maintain and repair pavements so that all who wish to use them have free passage. This duty to maintain may extend to the removal of snow and ice, as well as taking protective measures in bad weather. The law also, however, gives highway authorities a special defence in claims against them arising from, say, damaged pavements (Highways Act 1980, section 58), if they can prove that they have taken 'such care as in all the circumstances was reasonably required' to ensure that that part of the highway was not dangerous. In other words, as long as they have procedures for monitoring and repairing 'unsafe' pavements, and those procedures were in operation, they may have a defence against claims for damages, even though the pavement in question was dangerous.

Highway inspectors

One of the practices adopted by most local authorities to show they take all reasonable care to maintain their highways is to employ highway inspectors, whose main task is to locate areas needing basic maintenance. In response to a questionnaire which we sent to selected shire district councils on their highway maintenance practices, sixteen out of the nineteen councils replying employed highway inspectors. Their main functions are summarised in this fairly typical description from Rochester upon Medway City Council:

> "Routine inspection of all adopted highways and footways; assessment of condition of highway in relation to:
> - footways—trips, broken slabs, dangerous ironwork etc.
> - carriageways—cracking, polishing, rutting, drainage etc.
> - street lighting and other furniture
> - vandalism
> - accident remedial matters
> - insurance claims
> - public complaints
> Basically, the streets' inspectors are the 'eyes' of the office and so their brief is to inform and report and instigate (on a small scale) any related matters." (5)

We understand that a few authorities do not employ inspectors, because they claim they have insufficient funds to act on inspectors' findings. These authorities will be required to pay higher insurance premiums, because it would be more difficult for them to prove they had taken all reasonable care. We believe that it is quite unacceptable for footway conditions to be allowed to deteriorate to the detriment of pedestrian safety. Prevention of accidents must clearly take precedence over the provision of redress, and allowing resources to be pre-empted by insurance premiums, rather than pavement inspection, is not a priority that we would accept.

Standards

Another problem identified by the Standing Committee on Highway Maintenance was that of standards for footway maintenance (6). This can be traced back to the Marshall Committee on Highway Maintenance which reported in 1971. While the Committee had proposed fairly rigorous, quantified standards for carriageways, those for footways were much more vague, on the grounds that dangerous conditions were likely to vary according to circumstances and legal interpretation. The Marshall Committee had nevertheless suggested that the following conditions should be dealt with to prevent further deterioration and (in the words of the Committee) 'the likelihood of dangerous conditions arising':

★ projections and sharp edges more than 20mm (3/4in) high;
★ cracks or gaps between flags more than 20mm wide;
★ depressions more than 25mm deep;
★ rocking slabs;
★ loose stones on hard surfaces.

Apart from a requirement to repair or signpost potentially dangerous conditions as soon as they were reported, the Marshall Committee proposed simply that for shopping areas and town centres, there should be an annual programme of patching and resurfacing to keep the surface even and free of loose material and standing water, and for all other footways only the minimum of maintenance should be carried out, to keep them safe and free of standing water (7).

These 'standards' do not provide an adequate basis for undertaking footway repairs and maintenance. It is not surprising, therefore, that the Standing Committee on Highway Maintenance concluded that 'authorities rarely have a declared policy for footway standards; usually, they reach a consensus internally on what standards are compatible with the constraints of the funds available'. The Committee went on to say, however, that in none of the areas they looked at did the overall standards approach those implied by the recommendations of the Marshall Report. 'The funds available for maintenance' said the Committee, 'did not permit the attainment of such standards; which raises the question of whether the lower standards now achieved are in fact acceptable to the public, or whether resources made available are "inadequate"' (8).

The evidence we have collected about consumer concerns demonstrates most emphatically that the lower standards are not acceptable. We therefore endorse the efforts of the local authority associations to define standards more rigorously, as part of a *Code of Practice* on highway maintenance (9). The intention is to produce a common set of standards while acknowledging the need for flexibility to meet local conditions.

Two sorts of standards are proposed for footway maintenance: general failure conditions which will require repairs (fairly similar to those in the Marshall Report) and a set of footway warning levels requiring more extensive maintenance. (The *Code of Practice* also covers kerbs, snow and ice clearance, maintaining pedestrian crossings, road lighting and so on.)

Over-riding by vehicles

Ensuring that the resources devoted to footways are sufficient to maintain adequate standards should go a long way towards reducing the extent of natural deterioration. It is imperative to tackle the other two significant causes: over-riding, especially by heavy lorries, and problems caused by public utility operations.

The damage caused by over-riding can be tackled in two ways. Preventing over-riding through legal and other means, and by developing pavement surfaces that can withstand the effects of over-riding by heavy lorries. Leicester City Council told us that 'On all footways where footway damage by vehicles is prevalent it is now practice to strengthen the first metre behind the kerb edge with either deeper construction or stronger slabs (10).'

While we can sympathise with this approach, as a general principle we believe that pavements are for people. It follows that the priority must be to prevent vehicles encroaching onto pavement space. We must, therefore, ask whether the law on pavement driving and parking is adequate and—equally important—whether it is adequately enforced.

We believe that the police should devote more effort to enforcing existing laws. Although in certain cases drivers may have no option but to drive on the pavement, 'more commonly...over-riding is a matter of convenience rather than necessity' (11). Chief constables need to be convinced of the extent of public concern about driving (and parking) on pavements.

Equally importantly, physical enforcement could be greatly improved if highway authorities were to make full use of their powers to erect rails, fences and bollards, as well as traffic regulation orders (Road Traffic Regulation Act 1974), to prevent over-riding or pavement parking. Thamesdown's approach is to be welcomed:

> "Among some streets measures have been taken to provide a physical separation between vehicles and pedestrians, ie use of bollards. Whilst these have been provided as a deterrent against vehicle encroachment onto footways, they have a secondary benefit of protecting the pedestrian." (12)

Public utility street works

Finally, we turn to public utility street works, allowed under the Public Utility Street Works Act 1950 (PUSWA). As this Act was recently extensively reviewed for the Secretary of State for Transport (13), we limit our comments to some of the main points.

The problem can be simply stated. Public utilities—which means any authority that is statutorily obliged to provide services to the public, whether under private or public ownership—have to dig up roads and pavements to lay or gain access to their equipment. They do this all the time. In 1982/83, for example, it was estimated that the electricity, telecommunications, water and gas industries dug about two million holes in the roads and pavements in England and Wales (14). The gas industry alone was responsible for about half of these. Excavations weaken the fabric of the highway. If improperly signed, guarded or resurfaced they may constitute a hazard for pedestrians and road users. Moreover long delays can occur between temporary reinstatement (necessary to allow settlement) and permanent restoration. Although under PUSWA, public utilities must undertake a reasonable standard of reinstatement, highway authorities and the utility companies have constantly argued about standards and responsibility for particular reinstatements. A model agreement drawn up in 1974 attempted to resolve these differences—and set time limits on responsibilities of both highway authorities and public utilities—but the problems remained.

In 1983, the Select Committee on Transport identified three pressure points where the legislation was clearly not working (15). These were:

★ the quality of temporary reinstatements carried out by public utilities is often very poor;
★ there is often inadequate liaison between public utilities and highway authorities about the planning and timing of excavations;
★ highway authorities are having to bear additional road maintenance costs as a result of the damage caused by public utilities.

The PUSWA Review Committee was set up in response to the Select Committee's recommendations. Its report (the Horne Report) was published in November 1985. The Horne Report's principal recommendations were that the costs of public utility excavations should be fully borne by the utility companies, and that highway authorities should have greater powers of inspection and coercion to ensure that defective reinstatements are spotted and put right. New national specifications should be drawn up to cover materials, standards of work and performance and there should be 'guarantee' periods when responsibility remains with the utility companies. These central recommendations were accepted by government in July 1986 (16).

The report also made a number of recommendations about the signing and guarding of worksites, designed especially with the needs of blind and disabled people in mind, and about the need for better information for motorists and cyclists (though not pedestrians) about utility works to help them to plan other routes. The government response argues that action on this last recommendation should be left to highway authorities, as it is these bodies that deal with inquiries from the public. We hope that this will indeed be taken up by highway authorities, and improved information made available. We would add that such information must be aimed at pedestrians as well as other road users. Horne went on to recommend that '...the many interests involved should come together to work out how best this could be arranged.' We believe that pedestrians should be among the interest groups represented.

In general, we believe the Horne recommendations will lead to a much needed clarification of the responsibility for footway repair. In order to put them into practice, legislation is needed. We urge the government to bring forward such legislation as a matter of urgency.

While we generally support both the findings of the report and its recommendations, we would make the following observations. First, the Horne Report appears to suggest that while streetworks cause some inconvenience to the public at large, they constitute a danger largely to people who are blind and disabled. We believe this understates the problem and the widespread level of public concern. However, we accept that proposals aimed at helping the least mobile will be of benefit to all.

Secondly, the recommendations for better signing, guarding and lighting excavations are sound, but they must be properly enforced. Horne proposes that the police should be responsible for enforcing standards of signing and guarding (as they are, for example, for the lighting of builders' skips). The Association of Chief Police Officers, however, opposes this recommendation, believing that it should be a local authority duty. We are not particularly concerned who carries out this function, only that whoever is given the duty is willing to carry it out properly. We also believe that the proposals for signing, guarding and lighting utility streetworks should apply equally to highway authority worksites.

Thirdly, Horne proposes arbitration in cases where highway authorities and utilities cannot agree on whether a reinstatement is defective. The arbitration process must not be allowed to introduce delays.

Finally, the Horne Committee expressed its concern that some highway authorities have accepted that traffic cannot be kept off pavements and are proceeding, as a method of avoiding footway damage, to increase their strength by installing concrete bases, particularly under paved surfaces. It therefore recommends that highway authorities and utilities should 'reconsider the problem of vehicles damaging footways', with a view to finding a solution more acceptable to all. This rather weak recommendation reinforces our previous discussion about pavement parking and over-riding. In its response, the government argue that '...given the resource problems of implementing a general ban on pavement parking, no single solution may be possible'. On a more positive note, it goes on to suggest that highway authorities, utilities and the Department of Transport might 'explore the various possibilities either for preventing over running at pavements, or mitigating the consequences.' We hope that such discussions will be opened as soon as possible, with a strong emphasis on prevention rather than mitigation. The police, who have as important a part in these discussions as utility companies, should also be involved.

The role of public complaints

We have looked at the problems people face with damaged pavements. We now turn to the issue of complaints from the public, and the part they can play in improving conditions. In most cases, people who report pavement faults—including those involved in accidents—are not seeking retribution. They are much more likely to want two things:

(a) an apology—if appropriate—from the responsible body, and

(b) action taken to remedy the defect.

Time and time again this point was made to us, and some bitterness expressed at the dismissive or hostile tone met by members of the public reporting defects:

> "My secondary purpose in making this claim was to alert the various authorities to the dangerous condition of the pavements in this road but I have had no apology nor have the half hearted remedial works been adequate."

> "I was annoyed that my complaint was not acknowledged and that nothing was done to make the pavement safe..." (17).

The resentment created by a simple failure of councils to deal courteously with the public in complaints-handling is both unnecessary and against the councils' own interests. The public can and do act as unpaid pavement inspectors. This is borne out by the information provided by selected district councils for our own survey of footway maintenance procedures (18). We asked councils to list the main causes and numbers of public complaints about pedestrian matters received in 1985/86. In the fourteen who gave any breakdown, pavement damage featured throughout, although the categories used by councils varied, making it difficult to give comparisons of actual numbers or proportions of types of complaint. Middlesbrough gave a global figure of 3,741 complaints, Leicester mentioned 1,243 footway complaints, Three Rivers stated 41 (broken slabs, uneven pavements, pot holes, bad reinstatements), and Southampton estimated 1,000 on footway conditions and 500 on kerb conditions.

The 1980 national study of footway maintenance also mentioned the significant role of the public in notifying footway defects. The report noted that 'the general public is by far the biggest single source of complaints, accounting for between 60 per cent and 96 per cent of those received in the study areas.' At least two-thirds of sites reported in this way required treatment. Serious defects on busy footways were commonly attended to very quickly. In one study area, for example, about 20 per cent of defects were attended to within 24 hours, and just under half within five days (19).

In our own survey of selected district councils seven out of nineteen said that public complaints accounted for a half or more of all their basic footway maintenance jobs in 1985/86. In the other twelve councils, the proportions were given as between one per cent and a third of all jobs.

The speed of response to complaints varied enormously among these councils. Regrettably, our survey of district councils suggests that many councils fail to adopt a systematic approach to the reporting and analysing of public complaints. Fourteen said they had no special scheme for helping people to report pedestrian problems, and only six of the nineteen councils said that they recorded and analysed complaints received.

Among the examples of good practice, Middlesbrough, Rochester upon Medway and Southampton all operate 'postcard notification schemes'.

Rochester described their system:

"We have a 'complaint/suggestion' scheme in operation. Reply paid postcards are distributed to each house (with refuse sacks—every 20 weeks). Two cards per house. This means that about 110,000 cards are distributed with a response of between 3-4000 on average. The street inspectors then investigate *each* complaint and action and reply accordingly."

Southampton told us:

"the council introduced a postcard-reporting scheme in January 1985, known as OOPS. Cards are available through sub-post offices, doctors surgeries, community centres, cycle shops, and all council offices. About 6700 cards have been received to date."

Leicester adopt an even more comprehensive approach to complaints-handling. They reported:

> "our special scheme applies to everyone, not just pedestrians. We have a direct telephone line (listed in the telephone directory) to a Complaints Officer who sees that messages are passed to the relevant member of staff. Letters involving more than one type of complaint are handled by the Complaints Officer who co-ordinates the reply."

Leicester's scheme combines reporting, handling and analysis:

> "All complaints which are referred to the Complaints Officer are recorded, separated into type and sent to the appropriate section to deal with. On completion of repair, etc. details of the action taken are returned to the Complaints Officer to file."

Southampton also mentioned that their complaints records are referenced to detect a pattern of complaints, or the same defect reported by different people.

Having a scheme for encouraging the public to report complaints does seem to lead to a higher proportion of basic work being generated by such complaints, though the relationship is not entirely straightforward. The five authorities that had some sort of scheme reported an average of 50 per cent of basic repair jobs arising from public complaints, against an average of 31 per cent among those without such schemes. Of the six authorities with the highest proportions of jobs arising from public complaints, three had some form of reporting scheme. At the other end of the scale, nine out of nineteen authorities reported that 20 per cent or less of basic jobs arose from public complaints. Only one authority in this group had a reporting scheme (Middlesbrough, 20 per cent).

We warmly welcome these initiatives by councils which have changed the official attitude towards complaints-handling to one which sees public notification of problems as 'early-warning' messages rather than 'moans'. They have adopted a partnership approach with the public. We very much hope that other councils will follow suit. It should be noted that this approach places a greater obligation on a council to inform the complainant about the outcome, particularly if no action is taken arising from the notification.

Expenditure on pavement repairs

The funding arrangements for highway construction and repair are complex, and have been the subject of controversy in recent years. Essentially, the responsibility for setting priorities remains with the highway authority, though local authority expenditure is, of course, subject to central government limits. Nominally, the amount set aside for highway maintenance is agreed by a local authority and the Department of Transport as part of the grant related expenditure (GRE). However, in practice the Department insists that the amount actually spent on different services is a matter for the local authority. Transport supplementary grants (TSGs) are also available for '... capital expenditure which is of more than local importance. In particular, ... roads which form part of the primary route network of major through routes, important urban roads and bypasses and relief roads' (20).

In a study of road maintenance (including footways) carried out in 1982-83, the House of Commons Select Committee on Transport noted the near-unanimous agreement among the local authority associations and the professional engineering institutions that the current level of financial support for the maintenance of local roads was inadequate (21). Although the Committee recognised the difficulty of defining financial need in the absence of agreed maintenance standards (see below), the members went on to state their belief that:

> "the Government should take immediate steps to make additional resources available to local authorities for highway maintenance. Taking account of the backlog of maintenance works which has been building up, we believe that, as a minimum, a ten per cent real increase in expenditure on local road maintenance is likely to be required over several years in order to prevent further deterioration of the road network."

The Department of Transport has since increased the level of local road maintenance spending accepted for grant purposes, though this has fallen short of the amount local authorities said they needed. Road maintenance budgets were increased in the 1986/87 year. The government has claimed that this constitutes an increase of 15 per cent, though the House of Commons Select Committee has called this figure 'misleading', and the Institute for Highways and Transportation point out that a real reduction in the overall level of rate support grant has more than offset the increase in the highways element (22).

However, the expenditure on pavements is not necessarily determined by this overall figure. It is not easy to get reliable figures on how much is spent on footway maintenance. The Standing Committee on Highway Maintenance (SCHM) estimated in 1981 that some £50 million a year was spent on footway maintenance on non-motorway roads in England, or 10 per cent of all highway maintenance expenditure (23). This, they said, was equivalent to about £250 for each kilometre of footway. However, the Committee also noted the severe problem of common costs—work on the footway is usually done by the same roadmen as work on the carriageway, and administrative costs will also overlap.

Nevertheless, figures are published separately in the Standing Committee's *Annual Survey*. The accounting procedures used mean that the figures are broken down by road type. In most categories, the 1985 survey shows expenditure on footways faring relatively well in comparison with carriageway expenditure. On all classes of road, carriageway maintenance expenditure was at a low compared with its historical levels. By comparison, expenditure on footways has remained constant, and in the case of principal roads it is, if anything, above its historical level (24). However, this needs to be qualified in a number of ways.

Firstly, there are undoubtedly wide variations between authorities. In 1980, the SCHM found that in some local authorities the proportion of the highway maintenance budget spent on footways was as low as 0.7 per cent, and in others as high as 23 per cent. The Committee notes that '... authorities rarely make a specific decision about the total level of footway maintenance expenditure'.

Secondly, it must be borne in mind that a large part of the damage to pavements is caused by over-riding by vehicles. Although this part of the expenditure benefits pedestrians, it could be argued that it is effectively an addition to the carriageway budget, as it arises from the use of the pavement by motor vehicles.

Perhaps more importantly, the constancy in the expenditure figures may simply reflect a long-term underfunding of footway maintenance. The Standing Committee's study of footway maintenance reported that, in one of the areas studied, some 90 per cent of the footway maintenance budget was devoted to 'basic' as opposed to 'planned' maintenance, compared with an average of 50 per cent. The Committee pointed out that 'In the study authority which spent 90 per cent of footway resources on basic maintenance, a severe constraint on resources meant that priority had to be given to dangerous sites, leaving little for urgently needed planned maintenance work' (25).

In the National Consumer Council's own questionnaire survey of selected district councils, of the sixteen supplying figures, nine councils had spent over 50 per cent on planned rather than basic footway maintenance in 1985/86. The widest variations were Rochester upon Medway's 78 per cent planned expenditure compared with Cheltenham's 75 per cent basic. Nine councils told us that the proportions of planned to basic expenditure had not changed significantly over the past five years, while eight councils said they had changed. Rochester upon Medway had increased basic maintenance because of two exceptionally severe winters of frost, and Southampton had done so as a result of its postcard complaints scheme for public reports of defects. Charnwood on the other hand told us that with the changes in direct labour legislation, there was a need to be more organised and efficient, so more planned work was being undertaken.

While the SCHM found that 'the very long cycles of major maintenance ... suggest strongly that the level of planned maintenance is not adequate', they declined to comment on whether the level of footway standards in the study areas were acceptable, beyond noting that in none of the areas did the standards approach those suggested by the Marshall report. Instead, they felt that pavement standards were a question of public acceptability.

We would argue that our own research has now shown that, in general, pavement standards are not meeting public expectations—indeed that they are a cause of considerable public concern. It follows that we see a need for more spending on pavement maintenance.

We believe that such an increase could be justified economically, as well as on the basis of consumer concern. The Department of Transport applies costings to road accidents involving injury or damage, to produce an 'economic' case for road safety measures. Applying the same costings to pedestrian accidents in which individuals require medical treatment after falling over damaged pavements suggests that these accidents are costing perhaps £90 million a year in Great Britain. This is calculated from extrapolations of the MORI survey, which suggest that, among people aged 16+, 450,000 have suffered accidents on damaged pavements requiring medical treatment, at £200 each. This excludes accidents involving children under sixteen, and assumes people suffer only slight injuries, when at least some will be hospitalised or killed. The Department of Transport costing for more serious accidents, including those '....involving an overnight stay in hospital' is £8,282 (26). We do not believe that accidents can be assessed purely on economic grounds, but the figures do highlight the inadequacy of the amount of money currently spent on repairing and maintaining pavements.

Although the question of underfunding of road maintenance has been a live issue in the past few years, it is remarkable how little attention has been paid to the footway, as opposed to the carriageway. Although the Select Committee did, in 1982, take evidence from the Pedestrians' Association, the debate has been dominated by motor vehicle interests. Nor have the local authorities been quick to plead on behalf of pedestrians. Their evidence has been principally about the need for increased carriageway maintenance.

The Select Committee concluded that, '... within the field of road maintenance, the first priority for the Department of Transport and the local authority associations is the determination of appropriate standards' (27). That is even more essential for footway standards, and without it, any attempt to decide on the 'appropriate' level of expenditure is doomed to failure. We urge the Department of Transport to turn its attention to a much more precise definition of satisfactory pavement conditions—based on the views of the actual users. We would also suggest that the Select Committee should consider holding an enquiry, specifically into pavement conditions.

The consumer's responsibilities

Improved co-ordination and funding will not be sufficient, on its own, to guarantee an improvement in the provision for pedestrians. Throughout this report, we have stressed two themes. First, that those who provide services must continuously consult those who use them. Secondly, that those who provide transport services must be prepared to treat pedestrians as being equally important as road vehicles. But the rights of pedestrians can of course be actively promoted by pedestrians themselves. We have said that pedestrians often feature as victims, but this need not always be the case.

As well as acting as the eyes and ears of the council on footway conditions, concerned residents can also band together to assess conditions themselves. How some people have set about this is discussed further in Appendix C on Local Action. We are also issuing a handbook—*Pedestrians, an action guide*—to help people to undertake these assessments, and to ensure that their message is conveyed to the people responsible.

Groups and individuals should use the political process to communicate their concern, applying pressure at all the points that matter: parish council, district council, county/regional council, and nationally. It is particularly important to apply pressure to elected members of all tiers of local government, because they control the allocation of resources and must be convinced that people care about their pavements.

References to chapter 4

1. Standing Committee on Highway Maintenance, *National road maintenance conditions survey 1985*: report, Department of Transport, February 1986.
2. Standing Committee on Highway Maintenance, *A study of footway maintenance 1979-80*, December 1981.

3. Association of County Councils, Association of District Councils, Association of Metropolitan Authorities, *Highway maintenance: a code of good practice*, ACC, ADC, AMA, July 1983.

4. Standing Committee on Highway Maintenance, *op.cit.*, 1981.

5. National Consumer Council questionnaire to selected district councils, *The pedestrian environment*, June 1986.

6. Standing Committee on Highway Maintenance, *op.cit.*, 1981.

7. Report of the Committee on Highway Maintenance (Marshall Report) HMSO, 1970.

8. Standing Committee on Highway Maintenance, *op.cit.*, 1981.

9. Association of County Councils et al., *op.cit.*

10. See reference (5) above.

11. Standing Committee on Highway Maintenance, *op.cit.*, 1981.

12. See reference (5) above.

13. Department of Transport, *Roads and the utilities, review of the Public Utilities Street Works Act 1950*, HMSO, November 1985.

14. Department of Transport, *op.cit.*, November 1985.

15. House of Commons First Report from the Transport Committee, Session 1982-83, *Road maintenance*, vol. I, 28-I, HMSO, February 1983.

16. Department of Transport, *The government response to the Horne Report on the review of the Public Utilities Street Works Act 1950*, HMSO, July 1986.

17. Comments taken from National Consumer Council questionnaire survey of pavement accident victims, February 1986.

18. See reference (5) above.

19. Standing Committee on Highway Maintenance, *op.cit.*, 1981.

20. Department of Transport, Circular 3/84, para. 2.

21. House of Commons, *op.cit.*, 1983.

22. House of Commons, 3rd report from the Transport Committee, Session 1985-86, *The government's expenditure plans for transport, 1986-87 to 1988/9*, p.xx, p.87.

23. Standing Committee on Highway Maintenance, *op.cit.*, 1981.

24. Standing Committee on Highway Maintenance, *op.cit.*, 1986.

25. Standing Committee on Highway Maintenance, *op.cit.*, 1981.

26. Department of Transport, *Road accidents Great Britain 1985*, p.28, HMSO, November 1986.

27. House of Commons, *op.cit.*, 1983

Chapter 5
Towards a pleasing environment

Creating an environment for pedestrians that is safe and pleasant involves both positive and negative measures. On the one hand, it means designing pleasure and enjoyment into the environment, and on the other, it means stopping behaviour which makes the environment unpleasant.

Broadly, a pleasant environment for pedestrians is one which is:

★ free from conflict with vehicles (safety) and the unpleasant side-effects of traffic—noise, intimidation, airborne pollutants etc;
★ clean and visually attractive;
★ comfortable and convenient, with good walking surfaces, seats, stopping places, public conveniences and so on;
★ protected from the worst effects of the weather; and
★ personally secure.

Tom Walsh has described the kind of issues which planners and designers must consider.

> "Pedestrian facilities are often too late and too small. Simply adding seats and trees in tubs does not address the problem, it is merely cosmetic plastering of the problem, but a great deal would be gained by the imaginative grouping of street furniture for advertisements/information/flower beds/seats/lighting and litter baskets.
>
> Equally, excessive landscaping and planting is not always the answer, indeed it is often an apology or excuse for low quality spatial designs. Look at the great piazzas, for example the Grande Place in Brussels which has almost total absence of landscaping but is thronged with pedestrians. Heavy landscaping is only needed if the building environment is sterile.

Properly designed pedestrian facilities and space can attract children, mothers, older people, all of whom can quite happily indulge in a very favourable pastime of 'watching the others' We all do, we all enjoy it.

The pedestrian like a motor car needs servicing periodically i.e. he needs to rest and refuel—so design points at which he can stop and rest—he is not a continuous machine. Perhaps we should try to redesign into the pedestrian journey the things we all enjoy—flower sellers, street musicians—life. We need lateral thinking and perhaps more co-operation from the private sector to move away from established practices purely because they sell easily (1)".

Designing a good pedestrian environment is a highly complex and challenging task. In the next chapter we suggest ways in which the planning procedures—for land use, transport, and individual site plans— could be improved to take more account of the pedestrian. In chapter 7 we focus on the special hazards of road traffic.

In this chapter we discuss a range of specific environmental problems that our surveys have shown to cause distress to pedestrians. In some cases—for example pavement parking—the solution for pedestrians is clear. Often, though, the solutions are more complex: an environment that is made safe from road traffic may be thereby made more risky in terms of personal security; pedestrian zones with interesting layouts and pleasant street furniture may be virtually impassable for blind people; the clearing of all shop displays from the pavements will certainly improve pedestrian mobility, but may make the walk less interesting. We do not attempt to set out precise design guidelines— that is a matter for those who provide the facilities. What must be recognised is that complex problems demand complex solutions. They also demand a real process of consultation with the people who will use these facilities.

Preventing an unpleasant environment

Dog dirt

Of all the factors which can make an environment unpleasant, dog dirt is the one most universally condemned.

There are around six million dogs in Britain, most of them pets (2). Under the law it is an offence to allow an unmuzzled ferocious dog to roam, to fail to control a dangerous dog or to allow a dog to worry livestock. Owners must license their dogs (though at the time we went to press the licence was scheduled to be scrapped), put a collar and identity disc on the dog when out and not allow it off the lead on designated roads. In addition, the majority of local councils have bye-laws prohibiting the fouling of pavements and grass verges. Apart from licence evasion, these laws are seldom enforced. Costs of enforcement are high, councils lack staff with the necessary dog-handling skills, police have other priorities and environmental health officers do not have the powers to demand names and addresses from offending owners.

Dogs leave an estimated one million kilograms of faeces and four and a half million litres of urine on the surface of Britain each day (3). Especially at risk from this unpleasantness are small children, blind people, and disabled people using hand-operated wheelchairs. As well as the obvious offensiveness, there are considerable health risks.

In Britain, the estimated number of infections and diseases contracted from dogs include some 10,000 cases of campylobacter enteritis (the commonest reported cause of diarrhoea in this country), 2,500 cases of salmonellosis, and some 16,000 children are infected by toxocara canis, the common roundworm of dogs (3). In humans, the larvae migrate through the tissue, causing fever and malaise. In a small number of cases, according to the Toxocara Reference Laboratory, eye damage can occur in up to a hundred children a year (4). Other infections and infestations include yersiniosis, hydatid disease, tapeworms, leptospirosis, and pasteurella.

Over the last decade, many government departments, local authorities, representatives of environmental health officers, farmers, vets, postmen and women, the Post Office, RSPCA, National Canine Defence League and the League for the Introduction of Canine Control (LICC) have all lobbied parliament for more effective dog control measures to be introduced, with little success.

Recent debate has centred on the licensing system. Less than half the dogs in Britain are licensed, despite 3,000 prosecutions a year for licence evasion. The licence—at present 37p—brings in revenue of £0.9 million and costs £3.4 million to collect (2). A government working party on dogs, set up in 1974, had recommended that the annual licence should be increased to £5, and that the revenue should be devoted to providing a dog warden service. Responsibility for enforcement—except for rabies control—should be transferred to local authorities (5). None of the working party's recommendations has been implemented, except in Northern Ireland where the £5 licence is used to provide a district council warden service, and councils can issue fixed-penalty fines for minor offences.

In 1985, the Department of the Environment issued its consultation paper, *Dog Licensing: future arrangements in Great Britain* (2). The Kennel Club and PRO Dogs opposed the licence. The British Veterinary Association, the Institute of Environmental Health Officers, the

National Farmers Union, LICC and the Joint Advisory Committee on Pets in Society (JACOPIS: an organisation bringing together the Association of Metropolitan Authorities, veterinary associations, animal welfare bodies and the pet food manufacturers association), all asked for a higher dog licence and a universal dog warden scheme. In spite of these representations, the government announced in July 1986 its intention to abolish the licence.

Progress is, however, being made on the local authority front. The Home Office has permitted four local authorities to experiment with anti-fouling bye-laws (the 'poop-scoop' bye-laws) similar to the State of New York's Public Health Law 1301: the Borough of Gosport, Rochester upon Medway City Council, the London Borough of Barking and Dagenham, and North West Leicestershire District Council. The bye-law makes it an offence to fail to remove faeces deposited by a dog, and offenders can be fined up to £100 in the magistrates courts. In each authority, the schemes were preceded by massive publicity campaigns, the distribution of disposable scoops and training leaflets. Disposal bins were placed in all parks subject to the fouling ban. In Barking and Leicestershire, parks and playing fields only were designated. In Rochester and Gosport, towns with long experience of dog wardening, bans were extended to footways and verges (6).

Interim reports from all four authorities show the overwhelming success of the scheme (7). Dirt disappeared overnight. Very few dog-owners complained about the extra effort, and non-dog-owners asked for schemes to be extended to other areas (8). The authorities concerned have now all become proficient at estimating the bin space required and arranging frequent emptying. There have been some prosecutions but in general, the threat of prosecution combined with facilities for easy pick-up have encouraged dog-owners to clear up after their dogs.

Another approach adopted by some councils is to employ dog wardens. At the time of the Working Party on Dogs (1974-76), fifty local authorities employed wardens, whose function was to educate dog-owners, and bring prosecutions when education had failed. Others have since created dog warden posts, usually in the environmental health department. A few have subcontracted the work to specialist firms. A survey reported in *Environmental Health*, July 1980 showed at least 102 wardens employed and a JACOPIS Dog Warden Survey in 1983 showed at least 152 wardens employed.

Both studies suggested that wardens were popular with the public and the press and had made significant contributions to the control of strays and therefore to the control of attacks on people and road traffic accidents. There is some evidence that the presence of a warden results in less fouling of pavements but neither that nor publicity gets rid of the problem altogether.

We consider that the best way forward is to build on the success of the poop-scoop bye-laws so that there is a nationwide ban on fouling in public places. The extent of public concern about dog dirt, revealed by our surveys, suggests that action should be taken now.

Litter

Litter does not generate the same strength of feeling among pedestrians as dog dirt, but even so 17 per cent of respondents in the MORI survey viewed litter or uncleared rubbish as one of the main problems in their area (9). Around one-third of the sample considered that pavements and pedestrian areas in their neighbourhood were not very (25 per cent) or not at all (9 per cent) clean. There is obviously room for improvement.

Leaving litter in a public place is an offence under the Litter Act 1983, punishable by a fine of up to £400, but prosecutions are rare, and the Association of Chief Police Officers and the Metropolitan Police both suggested to us that this part of the Litter Act is virtually unenforceable.

There are two main ways of changing the individual's behaviour concerning litter. The first is to employ the deterrent effect with stricter penalties and enforcement. The Chairman of the Association of Chief Police Officer's Traffic Committee told us he would favour the introduction of a fixed penalty procedure to deal with littering (similar to the established system for parking fines).

The other approach is to create an environment which people do not want to litter, and to reawaken civic pride. The Keep Britain Tidy Group (KBT)—an independent organisation recognised by the government as the national agency for litter abatement—favours this second kind of approach. For local authorities KBT has developed the Community Environment Programme (CEP), a systematic means of improving the environment, particularly by reducing litter, designed to bring about a permanent change in attitudes and practices. The CEP has five main features:

★ identifying the *attitudes* and related behaviour which lead to littering;
★ identifying the seven main *sources* of litter, (two are by pedestrians and motorists);
★ encouraging local authorities to *review waste management services*;
★ *involving the community* in the programme; and
★ *measuring* the success of the programme's implementation.

The National Consumer Council has described the CEP's methods of measurement in our 1986 report on local government performance measurement (10). Refuse collection and street cleansing services were two of the local government services we selected to show how authorities can set 'consumer targets' and monitor their performance.

Along with action by local authorities to tackle the causes of litter, there is enormous scope for local people to tackle the problem themselves, and many local residents' and amenity groups have been instrumental in creating a more pleasing environment. Perhaps one of the greatest hurdles to overcome is a feeling that litter and a generally run-down environment is a problem to be dealt with only by the official bodies—'their' problem, not 'our' problem. The pedestrians who complain about litter are often the cause of it. Attempts to encourage residents to care for their neighbourhoods themselves and to alert authorities to particular problems must be encouraged.

Nevertheless, the principal responsibility must remain with official bodies. Waste from shops and businesses can often be a particular cause of problems—unnecessarily so, in many cases, as waste compactors could be used to reduce the bulk of the refuse. Facilities need to be provided to enable people to care for their immediate environment. This can range from the provision of litter bins in sufficient numbers and appropriate places, to ensuring that refuse collection services are capable of dealing with the volumes of rubbish produced.

Government policy towards the litter problem has been ambivalent. On expenditure grounds, the government has attempted to reduce levels of certain road-sweeping services. A Department of Transport code of practice on maintenance of trunk roads and motorways recommended that they should remove litter bins from all-purpose trunk roads, to encourage people to take their litter home with them (11). It also recommended that local authorities should not scavenge roads, sweep them, or remove litter from them.

On 14 July 1986, the Minister for Environment, Countryside and Local Government, William Waldegrave, announced in the House of Commons a new initiative with the twin aims of cleaning up the environment and creating jobs for unemployed young people under the community programme (12). Initially, work was scheduled to be concentrated in five areas:

★ greening the cities;
★ conserving the industrial heritage;
★ tackling litter;
★ helping tourists on the move; and
★ making more of nature.

To co-ordinate work, a new organisation was set up, called UK 2000, with Richard Branson, Head of the Virgin Group, in the chair. A number of national voluntary organisations agreed to act as agents in launching the scheme, including the British Trust for Conservation Volunteers, the Groundwork Foundation, the Keep Britain Tidy Group, and the Royal Society for Nature Conservation.

DoE grants to the co-ordinating board and the participating agents will amount to some £750,000 in 1986-87, and 'at least at that level' in the following two years. Around 5,000 jobs will be provided under the Manpower Services Commission's community programme, at a cost of some £22 million in a full year, but this is not new money, and the 5,000 jobs will come from a package of an additional 35,000 community programme places announced in the Chancellor's Budget speech for 1986. Nevertheless the initiative does represent a new focus which could prove valuable in harnessing the energy and enthusiasm of the voluntary sector.

Personal security

Personal security is an issue of increasing concern, and may, ironically, be put at risk by some of the measures intended to promote pedestrian safety in relation to road traffic. Underpasses and foot tunnels are a particular example of this conflict. Indeed, this very problem contributed to the failure of the world's first pedestrian foot tunnel, built under the Thames and completed in 1840: 'Although 50,000 people passed through in the first twenty-four hours, it quickly lost its charm and was taken over by whores and "tunnel thieves", a new class of criminal who hid in its arches and mugged passers-by beneath the Thames' (13). The tunnel eventually found a use as part of London's underground railway system. Recently, research into the physical design features that lead to particular housing estates being perceived as insecure has identified segregated pedestrian walkways as contributing to anonymity, lack of surveillance and proliferation of escape routes (14).

Holes, skips and cyclists....preventing obstructions

For the most part, the assortment of objects which obstruct the pavements are a source of nuisance and annoyance to people rather than a direct source of physical danger. However, for some of those who wrote to us, these obstacles instil real fear and even act as a deterrent to going out:

"I personally feel increasingly vulnerable when out walking.....Twice, when out with a pram I was almost knocked down by a cyclist...."

"May we put in a complaint to you about cars and cycles on the pavements. There is nowhere where a pedestrian can walk in safety."

"Children, youths and even mindless adults riding cycles on the pavement, making elderly people like me a bag of nerves."

And for those with a mobility handicap, including the elderly infirm, and disabled, obstructions are a real hazard:

"Another point which is annoying and dangerous is when cars park over half of the pavement leaving no room for wheelchairs (or prams) to pass through. One has to manoeuvre the chair off the kerb, out into the road, round the car, and back up the kerb. It's quite hazardous."

"For two years I was almost completely blind and even now I am only about 25 per cent sighted. I find the motoring fraternity completely thoughtless, arrogant, selfish and totally without care for the blind, incapacitated or otherwise handicapped pedestrians. The pavements and verges are there solely for convenience as parking grounds.... Local authorities are little better in regard to the blind in the way in which traffic furniture is placed on pavements—often in the centre of pavements where the blind are bound to come into collision. The service industries leave debris where the blind are bound to come to grief...."

"The problem of vehicles parked on pavements has meant difficulties with a pram or pushchair. Sometimes there is no option except to walk in the road which is dangerous...."

"At this time of year the hedgerows are all overgrown. This is a great hazard for me as I have to try to prevent my (16 month old) son from grabbing at all the brambles and grasses, not to mention having to duck some of the tree branches. I cannot step into the road as it is a far too busy dual-carriageway."

"... I'm almost blind, a widow aged 71. Two or three times I have been knocked about by teenagers cycling on our footpaths."

Pavement-cycling

This has been illegal since the 1835 Highway Act. According to the Department of Transport there are nearly 2,000 convictions annually for illegal cycling on footways and footpaths. The police do not find it easy to enforce the law, however, a state of affairs acknowledged by both the Metropolitan Police and the Association of Chief Police Officers (ACPO) in discussion with NCC. The problem, as the Metropolitan Police see it, is the practical difficulty of catching offenders. Chief Constable John Over, for ACPO, posed a more serious dilemma: enforcement would mean insisting on child cyclists using the road, at greatly increased safety risk to themselves. This dilemma was acknowledged by several of NCC's correspondents, but in many people's view it is increasingly teenagers and adults who seem to be pavement-cycling.

The recorded/proven danger to pedestrians from pavement cyclists is low. One commentator suspected serious under-reporting (15) suggesting that if, as the GLC had found, two-thirds of serious cycle/vehicle accidents were not reported, it was likely that even more cycle/pedestrian incidents went unreported. Our own (CA) survey showed that a little over one per cent of all pedestrian accidents had been caused by cyclists. Three-quarters of the victims had required no medical treatment. The main problem, however, appears to be the *fear* of accidents, particularly among the elderly.

Some effort has been made by government to tackle the problem of cyclists—who are themselves a vulnerable group in road safety terms. Local authorities may remove all or part of a footway (section 66/Highways Act 1980) and, in its place, construct a cycle track with or without a right of way on foot (section 65/Highways Act 1980). Since then, the idea of shared-use of pavements between cyclists and pedestrians has become more popular among councils in their efforts towards safer cycling.

Where a cycle-track or shared-use footway is authorised, it must be clearly signposted, and in 1986 the Department of Transport updated its advice to councils on this facility. The note admits that 'Allowing cyclists even limited use of facilities previously reserved solely for pedestrian use can be contentious' (16), and says 'It must be emphasised that there are no circumstances in which a general or widespread opening of footways and footpaths to use by cyclists would be acceptable'.

This advice note permits the use of a simple white line, or different-coloured surfaces, to distinguish between pedestrian and cycle sections of the pavement, or completely unsegregated facilities, where necessary. However, unsegregated facilities are restricted to areas of low useage.

The current policy of liberalising the circumstances where pavement-cycling is to be permitted fails to meet two important objections. Firstly, that on unsegregated or only visually-segregated pavements, pedestrians (especially the infirm or disabled) have *no protection* from cyclists, and therefore no way of reducing their fear about collisions.

Secondly, even if there is adequate signing of shared-use, there is no effective deterrent to pavement cycling elsewhere, because the law is often not enforced.

We accept that there is a real dilemma about child-cyclists, but do not think that the present approach serves the general interests of pedestrians unless proper attention *is* paid to enforcement more generally. A better approach in the medium term might be to reach local agreement, allowing child cyclists on pavements up to a certain age (say, ten years old), while enforcing the law vigorously for cyclists above that age.

Utilities, holes and scaffold

Building debris, scaffolding, skips and excavations for streetworks are common obstructions. Utility digging of the pavement is covered by the Public Utilities Streetworks Act (discussed in chapter 4). Apart from this, temporary and minor obstructions are lawful; anything else is not. Skips must be lit at night, and can be left only with the council's permission for a prescribed length of time.

Scaffolding which encroaches onto the highway (eg. street-level scaffold around buildings) can be put up only with the permission of the highway authority, which may impose such conditions as it sees fit—including adequate signing and guarding. Southampton Council told us about one initiative which we welcome. They explained that 'where permits are granted for placing building materials on the highway, they are not allowed to obstruct the footway. A deposit of £50 is held until all material is cleared from site, against any work the Council may need to do to ensure this and other requirements are met. Unauthorised deposits are removed.'(17)

Organisations representing people with disabilities made it very clear in evidence to the Horne Review that present arrangements for protecting pedestrians from pavement works are inadequate. It is generally accepted that they are, in any case, not always adhered to. Horne makes recommendations about signing and guarding these works which we believe should be adopted by law. Highway authorities should require similar minimum standards to apply to all building materials, debris and scaffolding on pavements (18).

Advertising boards and streetworks

It is very common, especially in local shopping parades, for the pavement to be used for small traders' advertising boards. It is also common practice for shops to extend their goods for sale onto the pavement. These obstructions are a particular nuisance and danger to the poor-sighted or blind, and other handicapped people. They are also, judging from our correspondence, viewed by many more as unsightly and unnecessary.

The general attitude of local authorities towards these street offences seems to have been largely of benign tolerance. Sometimes there may be genuine complications about prosecuting, when shop frontages are owned by the shop and are therefore not part of the public highway (even if they are to all intents part of the pavement). However, in most instances there is no such ambiguity: merely a poor appreciation by authorities and traders of the unpopularity and nuisance of these obstructions.

Thanks largely to the persistent campaigning of blind and disabled groups, some councils have decided to tackle the 'advertising board' problem. The Greater Manchester Council produced an extremely clear leaflet as part of a crackdown on display-boards. Hove Borough Council, with a large population of elderly and disabled people, has conducted an anti-streetwares and display-boards campaign of leaflets and warnings to traders; and has successfully prosecuted for obstruction. The council is now appointing a part-time official 'whose job will be to ensure that the pavements are kept as clear as possible' (19).

Pavement parking

Under the Highways Act 1835 it is an offence wilfully to ride, or wilfully to lead or drive, any horse, ass, sheep, mule, swine, cattle, carriage, truck or sledge on any footpath or causeway by the side of a road made or set apart for the use or accommodation of foot passengers. Because a 'carriage' was later defined to include a motor vehicle (and has also been extended to include a bicycle) this means that wilful *driving* on pavements by any vehicle is against the law. It is not, in the case of light vehicles, an offence simply to be *parked* on the pavement—though it is an offence to park a heavy commercial vehicle wholly or partly on verges or footways, except in certain defined circumstances, notably that the vehicle is parked for loading or unloading and not left unattended. Special pavement parking laws operate in the Greater London area, and it is everywhere illegal to park on the pavement when yellow line waiting restrictions are in force; or to leave a vehicle in a dangerous or obstructive position—on the pavement or on the carriageway. However, the law in this area is obviously in general unclear and inadequate to meet the problems of over-riding and pavement parking.

Heavy vehicles (including, reportedly, local authority service vehicles) do extensive surface and underground structural damage to pavements, creating the risk for pedestrians of tripping and falling. The more immediate problem for pedestrians is the obstruction to residential pavements from parked cars. Councils and police both seem virtually to have given up trying to prevent this. Thamesdown Borough Council wrote to us, for example, that

"...it is not unknown in the County of Wiltshire, for the Highway Authority to positively encourage vehicles to park on pavements either partly or wholly, where vehicular congestion would otherwise be a problem." (20).

Spelthorne Borough Council has proposed an explicit policy of pavement parking in its draft Local Plan of February 1986. In order to relieve problems of on-street parking in residential areas, explained the plan:

"The Borough Council will permit the parking of vehicles on footways within defined limits in the following instances:

1. In areas defined by the Borough Council where there is a shortage of off-street parking;

2. Where parking wholly within the carriageway would interfere unduly with traffic flow or make access for emergency services difficult;

3. Where such parking would leave adequate footway for pedestrians and would not prejudice their safety;

4. Where the footway is structurally suitable".(21)

In conversation with an official from the Council, it was further explained that they had no proposals for enforcement of a ban in non-designated streets, nor had they yet specified any streets where the 'pro-pavement parking' policy might apply although these would be 'exceptional'.

Among those councils more concerned about pavement-parking, the main difficulty of enforcement is the legal loophole in the 1835 Highways Act. This loophole was nearly closed in 1974 when the government passed a Road Traffic Act in which section 7 made parking on the footway a specific offence. Although this section was passed into law, it was left to the relevant Minister to decide when it should be brought into effect. Opposition from both police and local authorities to enactment at the time, restated in 1978, was grounded in fears over the prohibitive expense involved in implementing and enforcing the ban.

In their evidence to us, North Herts, North West Leicestershire, Thamesdown and Warwick councils all made particular reference to the problem, Warwick mentioning that their highway inspectors leave printed cards on the windscreens of offending vehicles, to point out the hazard caused.

The balance of opinion among councils does now seem to favour a tougher stand: the Association of Metropolitan Authorities and the Association of District Councils both favour some powers to ban pavement parking, but wish to be able to do this at their discretion in selected areas, rather than the more general ban currently on the statute book, which would allow councils to designate *exemptions* from the rule. The AMA periodically lobbies government for a selective introduction of banning powers; so far without success. The ADC maintains its long held position of opposing the 1974 statute on financial grounds.

There is one example of a pavement-parking ban in existence, however, implemented by the Greater London Council prior to abolition, under its own Act of Parliament (GLC (General Powers) Act 1974) and operating since January 1985. This law allowed borough council enforcement officers, as well as the police, to prosecute offenders; and the GLC undertook to cover the costs of prosecution for those boroughs which wanted this—removing the heavy financial disincentive of proper enforcement. The GLC scheme was introduced with a major publicity campaign which in itself was claimed to have made a substantial impact on all but the ten per cent of 'hard-core' pavement parkers. By October of 1985 the participating borough councils had issued a thousand prosecution notices, and police another five thousand (although this latter figure also included yellow line parking offences). Early reports from the GLC were cautiously optimistic, concluding in April 1985 that 'it is hoped that a high level of enforcement, reinforced by an extended publicity campaign on both television and radio will achieve a higher level of compliance and encourage "hard-core" motorists to break the habits of a lifetime' (22).

The GLC scheme prompted considerable interest from other councils (including Manchester, Maidstone, Brentwood, Darlington, Hereford, Tendring, Cleveland and Thurrock) who were considering trying to introduce similar bans through local legislation. Some London boroughs chose to continue using the 1835 legislation, which attracts a £400 fine for successful prosecution, as against the GLC's £50 maximum.

The GLC experience was not without problems, and it is clear that to achieve results is time-consuming and costly. Legal powers must be backed by the employment of enforcement officials, small-scale physical measures (eg. bollards, parking bays etc.), frequent high-profile publicity, and the finance to meet the cost of prosecution. A higher level of fine would defray some of these costs (though not for the councils themselves), and a reduction in pavement-parking long term would reduce pavement repair bills substantially. Beyond that, the social benefit to pedestrians would be enormous.

The growing enthusiasm of local authorities for greater banning powers is apparently not matched by the police. The Metropolitan Police, although co-operating with the GLC ban, were not at all keen on it, foreseeing an increase in obstruction from roadside parking, which would cause problems for road traffic generally and especially emergency service vehicles. Chief Constable John Over, for ACPO, expressed a personal view that the police might more readily prosecute pavement parkers if adequate provision were made for safe, cheap, off-street car-parking.

Nevertheless, there were 38,000 cases of footway driving dealt with by magistrates courts in England and Wales during 1985, but only 72 cases of HGVs parking on pavements (figures supplied by ACPO). Several police authorities have produced leaflets warning drivers against pavement parking. These can be left on the windscreens of illicitly parked vehicles, and are thought to be more effective than similar leaflets produced by other bodies, as they convey a clear implicit threat of possible prosecution.

Councils' efforts to clear pavement obstructions

The National Consumer Council sought more information from councils on their policies and practices over pavement obstructions, through our questionnaire survey to selected district councils. On the face of it, where highways inspectors are employed, their time seems to be well devoted to pedestrian matters. Five of the sixteen councils with highway inspectors said that they spent 70 per cent or more time on these matters, and in another seven it was at least half their time. Bournemouth Council operates rather differently, with a highway inspector who devotes 100 per cent time to pedestrian matters, plus three trench inspectors who each spend a fifth of their time. Pendle, East Yorkshire and Huntingdonshire do not employ highway inspectors.

However, when it came to tougher enforcement action, only one council, Three Rivers, had brought any prosecutions for pavement obstructions in the past two year—six (of which four were successful) in 1984/85; and Middlesbrough indicated that the police had made (unspecified) prosecutions for pavement parking and cycling; and Cheltenham simply informed us that all prosecutions were brought by police.

Although our small survey cannot claim to be representative, we have no reason to believe that these councils' practices are untypical. The apparently very low level of council enforcement activity, compared with the amount of time devoted to pedestrian matters by inspection officials, is a sad reflection on the fact that most effort is having to be put into limiting the damage to pedestrian facilities caused by other road-users, rather than effecting real and significant improvements in pedestrians' environment.

On a more promising note, Middlesbrough Council sent us a copy of a new advice booklet, *Unseen Hazards*, which they are issuing to all public utilities, council and county council employees, shopkeepers, architects and other interested bodies. It is an attractive publication which combines clear and detailed advice on duties and precautions to be taken by all those involved in construction, digging-up, placing things on, above or near pavements.

The various obstructions mentioned in this chapter are a source of widespread annoyance, frustration and nuisance to pedestrians, in addition to the perceived or actual danger they pose. We believe that there is significant discontent caused by a perceived unwillingness on the part of the police and local councils to take action.

In the case of building debris, public streetworks, traders' goods and boards, or indeed street furniture, the problems can be blamed on official thoughtlessness (and personal thoughtlessness by the individuals or shop owners who clutter up the pavements). In the case of pavement cycling and parking, the interests of pedestrians are counterposed against those of the cyclists or car owners, and the latter seem invariably to win out.

What is lacking is any measure of consensus among the key agencies—councils, police and government—who could between them clear the pavements. In our view the basis for consensus is obvious and unchallengeable: pavements should be for people who walk. If the service-providers or law-enforcers think otherwise, they should justify their position and ensure that adequate *additional* provision is made, rather than the constant encroachments into walking space which are tolerated, and even encouraged, at present.

Creating a pleasant environment

Much of the rest of this report presents a rather gloomy picture of the experience of being a pedestrian, and our focus is often on removing or mitigating some of the worst aspects of the disadvantage that pedestrians suffer. At its best, though, walking can be a positively pleasant experience. Sometimes, the creation of pleasant walking conditions requires little human intervention. In other cases, major design and management efforts are required. The main problem, particularly in urban areas, must be to resolve the conflict between pedestrians and motor vehicles, not only in terms of pedestrian safety (see chapter 7) but also in terms of an attractive and comfortable pedestrian environment.

Most of the schemes aimed at resolving this conflict in favour of the pedestrian involve the segregation of pedestrians and vehicles though, more recently, there has been increasing interest in the Dutch system of 'Woornerven' in which pedestrians and vehicles share the same street surface. The latter approach has particular relevance in residential areas, and is based on the belief that '...communal and individual activities should be possible in residential areas' (24).

A much more widely adopted, and therefore better evaluated approach in the UK is the 'pedestrianisation' of town centres and shopping areas. This can range from the restriction of traffic in a single street to the very extensive town centre schemes in Bologna, Gothenburg, Munich and Vienna.

In part, these schemes simply remove the environmental hazards and unpleasantness created by motor vehicles. They remove the physical danger and intimidation caused by speeding vehicles, reduce noise levels significantly and reduce local concentrations of the range of air pollutants that internal-combustion engines emit (including carbon monoxide, hydrocarbons, fine particulates and oxides of nitrogen). This alone would be a significant gain for pedestrians.

Beyond that, though, the removal of vehicles opens up the possibility of creating an actively pleasant space for walking, sitting and shopping. As Brambilla and Longo have pointed out, a successful pedestrian mall should go beyond the alleviation of urban problems, with the aim that '... people will come to the mall for what it offers, not because there are only unsatisfactory alternatives.' (25) The physical possibility of creating an appealing environment is helped by the fact that the sort of road surfaces, lighting levels and road-signs that are appropriate for pedestrian areas are different from those required by motor vehicles. In many older British towns, the requirements of pedestrians match the grain of the existing townscape much more closely.

The benefits of pedestrianisation cannot be taken for granted: they should be quantified for each scheme. Not all are equally good, but Durham City Council's review of its pedestrianisation scheme shows how great the benefits can be (26). For example, the review noted:

★ an overall increase of 37 per cent in the number of pedestrians using the city centre, since pedestrianisation;

★ no significant change in the pattern of use, but an increased awareness of the historic environment of the city 'possibly because of the
better opportunity given to observe the surroundings';

★ better servicing for shops after pedestrianisation (although theoreti-
cally all shops had enjoyed unlimited front access for servicing prior
to the scheme, in practice it could only take place in the few areas
wide enough to allow vehicles to pass);

★ a 97 per cent satisfaction level among businesses in the affected
area;

★ a better physical environment: the amount of lead in the air had
dropped from a level approaching maximum to negligible, and noise
levels—previously eight times the acceptable level—had dropped to
well within the acceptable level of 68db;

★ a 400 per cent drop in the number of accidents involving pedestrians,
though accidents involving vehicle damage only remained fairly
high;

★ no apparent loss of trade: of the 100 traders replying to a questionnaire circulated in 1979, 52 reported an increase in trade, 31 believed
trade to have remained the same, and only 3 registered a decrease
(14 traders did not answer this question);

★ 85 per cent satisfaction with the convenience of bus stops among
users.

Given these recorded benefits, it is not surprising that TEST commented: 'Durham's centre changed over five years from a dangerous,
highly congested, and environmentally decadent area to one where, on
the peninsula and its bridges and the new shopping centre, it is a
delight to walk, shop, and admire a townscape of distinction' (27).

A good pedestrian environment is not solely a product of physical
design. The maintenance and management of the pedestrian zone is
equally significant. Most notably, even well-designed shopping centres
reduce rather than enhance the welfare of pedestrians if their managers
choose to lock the centre outside shop-hours. However understandable
this might be from the point of view of the operators, it has the effect
of creating 'no-go' areas, often in the core of the town. Less dramatically,
'... whether or not street vendors are allowed, sitting and strolling
encouraged, fund raising permitted, will affect who frequents a pedestrian area and why' (28).

Perhaps the most celebrated example of a lively pedestrian space in
Britain is the Covent Garden market, and it is also an early example
of a scheme in which participation by the local community helped to
shape the outcome. Original plans for the area, drawn up in the early
1970s, involved a comprehensive redevelopment plan that would have

swept away much of the existing architecture (though not the market building itself). However, the early 1970s saw a public loss of confidence in this sort of planning, and an associated growth of community action groups, among them the Covent Garden Community Association. These groups insisted on participating in the planning process and, as Geoffrey Holland, the Chief Planner of Covent Garden noted '... participation led inexorably to conservation' (29). The preserved and pedestrianised central piazza has become not just a lively shopping area, but a centre for street performers.

This range of potential—from tackling urgent problems of urban decay to creating a positively joyful environment—can be illustrated by quoting from two books, the conclusions of which are closer than these quotations may suggest:

> "Pedestrian malls are not urban idylls created in an artist's eye, but practical solutions to some urgent problems." (30).

> "In any place unrestrictedly set aside for walking we are free to be random, and silly, if we wish. The ultimate achievement would be to turn over a high proportion of urban movement space to walking, people in wheelchairs, shops, cafes, roller-skating and roller-coasters, processions, bazaars, tattoos, kicking footballs, circuses, Ferris wheels, perambulators, experimental buildings, sound and light shows, sand pits, solar collectors, buskers, food growing, sculptures, sheep grazing, exhibitions, trees, expanses of water, Punch and Judy, brass bands, flower sellers and school crocodiles."(31)

References to chapter 5

1. Tom Walsh, *Designing for the pedestrian journey in newly developing areas,* paper presented to a conference on Providing for the Pedestrian organised by Cheshire County Council, 22 April 1986.
2. Department of the Environment, *Dog licensing: future arrangements in Great Britain,* consultation paper, Department of the Environment Air and Noise Division, 1985.
3. D. N. Baxter, 'The deleterious effects of dogs on human health: Paper 2: canine zoonoses', *Community Medicine,* Vol.6, 1984, pp.185-197 and 'Paper 3: Miscellaneous problems and a control programme', pp.198-203.
4. G. H. Ree et al, 'Toxocariasis in the British Isles 1982-83', *British Medical Journal,* Vol.288, 25 February 1984.
5. Department of the Environment, *Report of the Working Party on Dogs,* HMSO, 1976.

6. R. L. Leather, 'It's a dog's life keeping areas clean', *Municipal Journal*, 4 April 1986, p.546.

7. Rochester upon Medway City Council, Housing Policy and Environmental Services Committee, *Dogs clean-up scheme—second interim report*, City Housing and Environmental Department, 13 January 1986.

8. London Borough of Barking and Dagenham, unpublished report to Parks Committee, *Poop scoop scheme*, 1985. Details from Chief Environmental Health Officer, Civic Centre, Dagenham.

9. Market & Opinion Research International, *Pedestrians*, summary report prepared for National Consumer Council, MORI, February 1986.

10. National Consumer Council, *Measuring up: consumer assessment of local authority services, a guideline study*, NCC, 1986.

11. Department of Transport, *Motorway and all purpose trunk roads*, code of practice for routine maintenance, 1985.

12. *Hansard*, 14 July 1986, cls.. 683-689.

13. R. Trench and E. Hillman, *London under London*, John Murray, 1985.

14. Peter Walters, 'The Mozart Estate, City of Westminster', *Housing Review*, Vol.35, No.5, Sept.-Oct. 1986.

15. J. Landles, GLC Transportation Department, in discussion with NCC, March, 1986.

16. Department of Transport, *Local transport note 2/86 Shared use by cyclists and pedestrians*, p.1, Department of Transport, August 1986.

17. National Consumer Council, questionnaire survey of selected district councils, *The pedestrian environment*, June 1986.

18. Department of Transport, *Roads and the utilities, review of the Public Utilities Streetworks Act 1950*, November 1985.

19. Michael Ray, Director of Planning, Hove Borough Council, in letter to NCC, March 1986.

20. David Kent, Chief Executive, Thamesdown Borough Council, in letter to NCC, April 1986.

21. *Spelthorne Borough Local Plan*, Policy M15, Spelthorne Borough Council, February 1986.

22. Report from Controller of Transportation and Development, *GLC (General Powers) Act 1974—Section 15 Pavement parking ban monitoring report and further exemptions on metropolitan roads*, Greater London Council, April 1985.

23. Middlesbrough Borough Council Engineering Department, *Unseen hazards*, Middlesbrough Borough Council, August 1986.

24. Royal Dutch Touring Club and Ministry of Transport and Public Works, *Woornerf*, The Hague 1980.
25. R. Brambilla and G. Longo, *For pedestrians only—planning, design and management of traffic-free zones*, Whitney Library of Design, New York, 1977.
26. *Durham City pedestrianisation scheme*, Report of the Durham City Pedestrianisation Joint Working Party of the Council of the City of Durham, Durham Constabulary and the Durham County Council, November 1982.
27. Teresa Ryszkowska, Jonathan Wade and John Roberts, *Solutions to problems of pedestrians crossing roads*, a report by TEST for the National Consumer Council, July 1986.
28. R. Brambilla and G. Longo, *op.cit.*
29. Quoted in Stephen Wood, *A tale of two markets*, Proceedings of the PTRC Annual Summer Meeting, July 1981, Planning and Transport Research and Computation (International) Co Ltd.
30. R. Brambilla and G. Longo *op.cit.*
31. John Roberts, *Pedestrian precincts in Britain*, Transport and Environment Studies, 1981.

Chapter 6
Planning with pedestrians

We are not professional planners, and this chapter is not intended to be a design manual on planning for pedestrians. Instead, we focus on the way that the planning process does—and does not—take pedestrian needs into account. Because pedestrians do not require hugely expensive facilities, their needs are very easy to overlook, particularly at the strategic stages of physical (land use) planning and transport planning.

Of course, in some parts of the country a great deal is being done for pedestrians. Town centres are pedestrianised, new housing estates are designed with pedestrian safety as a primary consideration, new pavement surfaces are developed to aid people with mobility handicaps, and so on. But too often these are isolated examples, improvements at the margin rather than evidence of a consistent concern to treat pedestrians and cars as equals.

This lack of consideration stems as much (if not more) from political will as from professional judgement. Those European countries that provide most generously for pedestrians do not always use economic criteria such as the cost-benefit of time saved to balance the needs of pedestrians and cars. In commenting on the contrast between provision in different countries, Hitchcock and Mitchell of the Transport and Road Research Laboratory (TRRL) speculate that 'what differs perhaps is the political perception of the importance of foot traffic' (1).

This chapter, then, is primarily about changing the political and professional climate within which both physical and transport plans are made. We look at the aims of planning and the problems people face now, then at the changes we would like to see introduced to the planning process. We deal separately with public consultation (for structure/local planning, development control, traffic measures and public inquiries), then look at some specific issues concerned with the development of new sites, the adaptation of existing areas—including pedestrianisation—and planning for people with mobility handicaps. We end with some suggestions for raising awareness of pedestrian needs.

The aim of planning

Bearing in mind that we are all pedestrians at least some of the time, the aim of planning for pedestrians must be to allow everyone to meet as many of their daily needs as they wish to on foot. This involves two levels of the planning process: in designing pedestrian *routes* that are safe, convenient and pleasant; and in planning the *location of facilities* so that they are reasonably accessible on foot.

These two planning levels are essentially complementary, and neglecting either can undermine the best intentions of the planners. The new towns, for example, have a reputation for pioneering work in the provision of segregated pedestrian routes. Yet at the larger scale they have been planned principally for those with access to a car. Milton Keynes provides a good illustration of the resulting conflict. In Stephen Potter's words:

> "... the Plan for Milton Keynes incorporated the goal of 'Provision for free and safe movement as a pedestrian'. Hence a network of segregated footpaths and cycleways. However, the density of development, land use patterns and distribution of facilities available at the mezzo-scale [the sort of journeys that can be made by pedestrians] are poorer than in most newly developed areas and considerably poorer than in existing cities."(2)

Equally, planners must recognise that their designs can only work if people like them enough to use them. Designs that are safe may not necessarily be convenient. Pedestrian subways and road-bridges are, in principle, safer than surface-level crossings, but may also be so inconvenient and uninviting that pedestrians avoid using them. In practice, therefore, they can end up creating more danger than they remove, as significant numbers of people choose to take their chances dodging between the cars on the road itself.

Planning for whom?

Evidence suggests—perhaps not surprisingly—that people undertake longer journeys on foot when conditions are pleasant. It is not just obvious things like rough terrain or a lack of direct routes that affect the distances walked; it appears that people will walk further in town if the surroundings are made visually attractive (3).

However, pedestrians have a great capacity to adapt to what is given and may not be conscious of restrictions on their mobility. In the MORI survey (reported more fully in chapter 2), we asked people if they were prevented from making any particular journeys on foot because of conditions for pedestrians. (Interviewers first asked people about the frequency of walking trips to various destinations (different kinds of shops, schools, work, recreation centres, pubs, walking for leisure etc.), and then asked: 'Are there any of these trips that you do not make on foot at present, but *would*, if conditions for pedestrians were better?') Only four per cent named specific journeys they would make if conditions were better, though the figure was higher among people who had had an accident in the previous year (six per cent), or had made a complaint about pedestrian conditions (eight per cent). Half of those questioned did not feel that they were being prevented from going anywhere on foot. However, a further 45 per cent—a very high proportion—gave no opinion (4).

Among those who did feel prevented from making particular journeys, the main reasons were: the volume of traffic (15 per cent), lack of time (12 per cent), lack of open spaces or parks (7 per cent), the cold weather (7 per cent), injury or ill health (6 per cent) and fear of mugging or attack if out alone at night (6 per cent).

Our survey specifically excluded distance as a possible reason for not making journeys on foot. However, the distance between residential areas and major communal facilities is clearly one of the main ways in which planning affects people as pedestrians. S.W. Town has suggested that poor access occurs for several reasons:

"Firstly, in the planning of certain facilities in the public sector, economies of scale have outweighed criteria of user access; a clear example of this is the case of hospitals. Another example would be the steady growth of school size, where considerations of educational efficiency may outweigh the increased journey lengths involved. Secondly, there are those facilities, the dominant users of which have access to cars, and which are located on the assumption that most of their users will have cars."(5)

Market forces are pushing the private sector in the same direction, for example in the growth of hypermarket developments and edge-of-town shopping centres at a time when, for many types of shopping, the number of retail outlets is declining steadily.

Access to shops for people without cars is often thought of as a rural problem, but its significance in urban areas was shown by a qualitative study of the shopping needs of inner city consumers, conducted by Market Behaviour Ltd on behalf of NCC:

"Many respondents mentioned problems with shopping that related to *getting around easily*, things that annoyed them and made it harder to shop. One of the most important needs seemed to be *proximity*: that a good shopping area, supplying most basic needs, with reasonable selection and prices, was within close walking distance. This seemed to be preferably within five minutes walk or at the most ten minutes. A walk longer than that was considered inconvenient, even though many did walk longer to achieve better prices and selection."(6)

A preoccupation with the needs of car drivers can leave pedestrians with conditions that are inconvenient, unpleasant, unsafe or insecure (or perceived as being insecure). At worst, it can lead to 'community severance', when neighbourhoods are cut in two by the volume of traffic on a major route. The damaging effect of this on a neighbourhood has been documented in various studies (7). A graphic illustration is provided by Marianne Hood in evidence to a public inquiry on London's North Circular Road:

"It was only after the event that (local people) realised how bad it was...It wasn't until people had been killed trying to cross because they were frightened of using high footbridges, and tried to cross at the easiest point on the road that we realised it was vital to have safe crossings for pedestrians that they could use. It wasn't of course until people started to say there was no point in trying to go to the library or the Welsh Harp because you can't get across the road.

Pensioners, people with babies and people who were handicapped, stopped using buses because they couldn't get to the bus stops on the opposite side of the road. We realised the effect the road was having—it was literally cutting the borough in two. In fact, the Department of Transport quite happily announced that they foresaw that in a certain number of years time, it would be two totally separate communities on opposite sides of the road. But this was really overlooking the fact that people still lived there. There didn't appear to be any plans to knock the houses down, although we never did get to see the feasibility study, and we have always wondered whether someone with a little more humanity had suggested that maybe all the houses should have been knocked down." (8)

The conditions described by Marianne Hood are extreme, but at a less dramatic level, the sorts of problems she describes are widespread. They stem, we believe, from the lack of attention given to pedestrian needs. Tom Walsh, Chief Engineer of Warrington and Runcorn Development Corporation, categorised the legacy of designers' insensitivity towards pedestrians as follows:

"inadequate footpaths in terms
of   width
     convenience
     obstructions
     signing

unpleasant footpaths in terms
of   discontinuity
     kerb heights
     lighting
     street furniture

hostile footpaths in terms
of   vandalism
     crime
     fear, real or imagined

dangerous footpaths in terms
of   tripping
     congestion
     adjacency to traffic
     conflict with traffic

no footpaths whatsoever in many cases."(9)

While agreeing that there are now numerous schemes favouring pedestrians in shopping areas, Hitchcock and Mitchell argue that pedestrian convenience is often given a low priority in schemes to improve the flow of motor traffic. They point out that:

"the single step that would achieve a better balance for pedestrians in new schemes would be action based on recognition of the facts that it is physically easier for motor vehicles than pedestrians to change level or travel additional distance to aid segregation, that motor vehicles protect their occupants from the weather, and that pedestrians appreciate a pleasant environment."(10)

These kinds of consideration perhaps explain why pedestrians—unlike the planners and engineers who design for them—often value their convenience more highly than their safety.

The planning process—and how it could be improved

(a) Structure plans, local plans and transport plans

Structure plans are meant to deal both with improvements in the physical environment and with traffic management schemes, and might therefore be expected to include strategic statements about provision for pedestrians. In practice they rarely do.

Transport policies and programmes are another obvious place in which to set out details of pedestrian schemes, and indeed transport authorities have been specifically asked to use the plans in this way. We understand that the information supplied has been disappointing. Certainly the recent TPP documents we have seen pay only cursory attention to pedestrians, generally by reference to pedestrian safety and the development of pedestrian precincts. Pedestrians rarely feature among authorities' primary objectives.

Structure plans are strategic land-use planning documents prepared by upper-tier or single-tier local authorities and approved by the Secretary of State for the Environment, Wales or Scotland. The first round of plans were prepared in the 1970s. Most plans cover a period of ten to fifteen years, so many authorities are now considering revisions to their strategic plans which will take them into the 1990s and beyond.

Local plans are usually prepared by lower-tier district councils, following a development plan scheme established by the upper-tier authority. They are of two main types: general plans cover a range of subjects, but only a limited geographical area—perhaps a single town; subject plans cover a single topic, and would usually deal with a larger geographical area. Again, most of the first generation of local plans has been produced, although they are kept under continuous review.

Under the Local Government Act 1985 the metropolitan areas of England and Wales will have to produce new plans for their areas called *unitary development plans*. These will combine the strategic aspect of the structure plan with the detailed proposals of the local plan. But no date has been set for this—the Department of the Environment is still working on the preparation of guidance and regulations, though some councils are already liaising with the Department's regional offices.

Highway authorities in England and Scotland must also pro-duce annual *transport policies and programmes* (*TPPs*) for the Secretary of State for Transport or for Scotland. These cover a rolling five-year period. Authorities have recently been asked by central government to include in their TPP a statement of what they are doing for pedestrians.

Local plans are even more important in the provision of pedestrian facilities, for it is at this level that the service must actually be delivered. Some are already extremely thorough in the attention they pay to pedestrians. We were sent a number of examples, following the circulation of a note about our work by the Association of District Councils. Derby City Council, for example, devoted a section of its local plan to pedestrians, noting that many of its general proposals were aimed at improving pedestrian safety and making the City Centre a more pleasant place, but suggesting a number of further, special measures. The plan states that:

> "the City Council will seek to ensure the development of a number of pedestrian priority routes, incorporating pedestrianised streets. Urban squares and other informal public open spaces will be developed at appropriate points on these routes."(11)

The pedestrian priority network is to be created gradually, for example by use of the conditions attached to planning permission. Other proposals include the creation of a walkway on both sides of the River Derwent; the development of a safe and pleasant pedestrian link between the railway station and the central area; 'tidy up' exercises and tree planting on public land; and the incorporation of canopies and colonnades into future retail and associated developments, to protect pedestrians from the weather.

Derby City's plan stands out because it pays attention both to strategic needs and to the finer details of planning and design which can make life more pleasant for people walking through the city's streets. Derby's is not, of course, the only example of good pedestrian planning, and district councils often view criticism of their concern for walkers as unfair. Oxford City Council, however, sent us a copy of its local plan which amplifies the point:

> "The importance of walking and cycling has tended to be neglected perhaps because the formulation of transport policy has largely been a problem solving activity and walking and cycling have not caused many problems (except for the number of accidents involving pedestrians and cyclists and these are generally the fault of other road users)."(12).

Some 40 per cent of all journeys in the Oxford study area were made exclusively on foot or by bicycle. The council observe that if 40 per cent of the transport budget were devoted to pedestrians and cyclists, whatever problems they had would disappear.

Many of the plans sent to us by district councils were impressive, but there were generally two omissions: councils rarely seem to collect information directly from pedestrians themselves about their needs; and few councils appear to have developed strategic plans that would lead to the creation of a network of routes.

(b) Giving pedestrians greater priority

We suggest three main improvements in the way land use and transport plans are produced.

First, authorities should collect much more information about the needs of pedestrians in their area, to provide a basis for political decision-making about the relative priorities of different road-users. Many commentators have noted both the need for such information, and its relative rarity. Hitchcock and Mitchell observe that:

> "there do not seem to be any formal schemes of assessment, either of priorities on maintenance or design of schemes, which take account of pedestrian needs relative to those of other road users, or even assign priorities to different pedestrian problems, though it is claimed that the proposed schemes for trunk roads will do this. Nor, in general, is there adequate objective data to predict the demand for walking and to enable any such assessment technique to be applied (taking account of the fact that many pedestrians do find difficulty in walking, or are encumbered with goods)."(13)

Techniques for collecting information about pedestrians are already well developed. Alan McMillen, Senior Planning Officer for Barnsley Metropolitan Borough Council in the 1970s, describes two that were used in the formulation of Barnsley's local plan: a *conflict* survey, based on observation techniques, to count the number of pedestrians crossing roads and walking along pavements, and for pedestrian delays and crossing times; and a *route* survey, based on interviews, to establish the routes pedestrians took around the centre (14).

Secondly, we would like to see district councils preparing pedestrian movement plans, particularly for urban areas. The approach at present relies too heavily on the creation of pockets of pedestrianised areas, with little attempt to link these pockets into a network. Pedestrian movement plans would examine the journeys people currently make on foot and so help to pinpoint particular problems such as congested pavements or long delays to cross roads. They would also look at the journeys people would like to make, so that authorities can develop a strategic plan for pedestrians, and consider how future developments might aid or hinder pedestrian movements. Once the plans have been developed, annual checks must be carried out to monitor specific problems. York City Council told us it was about to embark on a

Visitor Study which will include examination of the movement of large volumes of people to and from the City's shops and tourist attractions (15). We would like the residents and workers of all our towns and cities to benefit from this kind of consideration.

Thirdly, new planning development proposals should be accompanied by a 'pedestrian impact statement'. Except for planning permissions for wholly private domestic premises, all other proposals should include an analysis of the effects of that development on the safety, convenience and pleasantness for pedestrians. In major new developments these implications should be considered both for the local population and those who are intended to visit/use/work at the new site, for example shopping schemes, factories, hospital reorganisations and particularly school closures and amalgamations. Alan McMillen has argued that it is essential to ensure that measures to assist the pedestrian are not merely a spin-off from proposals designed primarily to ease traffic congestion, but take full account of the likely benefits to pedestrians (16). Ways of improving the safety and convenience of children on their journey to school have been clearly identified by Walsh for both new developments and schools in existing areas (17). His approach is vital at the earliest planning stages.

These three developments—more research and analysis, pedestrian movement plans and pedestrian impact statements—are relevant to local authority planning and highways/transport departments. Because so many pedestrian problems can be traced back to an imbalance in their treatment compared with other road users, we would welcome the creation of 'pedestrian units' within highways or transportation departments of upper-tier authorities; and within district councils, spanning both engineering and planning departments. Their brief should be wide-ranging: to research, propose plans and monitor schemes designed to promote the safety, convenience, security and pleasantness of the pedestrian environment. Similar units should be established within central government.

Our proposals echo the kind of approach outlined in a recent code of practice on highways and traffic management in London, prepared by the Association of London Borough Engineers and Surveyors in co-operation with the Department of Transport (18). An extensive chapter of the code is concerned with 'Helping Pedestrians'. It recommends careful consideration of pedestrian movements, and suggests how innovative approaches may be possible in areas undergoing major redevelopment. Most of the time, however, the code recognises that helping pedestrians means solving specific problems which generally concern some form of conflict between pedestrians and vehicles. The code proposes that pedestrian needs should be considered on an area basis, rather than solely at isolated sites, and provides practical advice on identifying and classifying problems, investigative methods, consultation, and measures to assist pedestrians.

(c) Consultation with the public

We deal here with two sorts of consultation: first, consultation about general plans for the future; and second, consultation about specific issues. Both are provided for within our legal system.

The Town and Country Planning Acts established a fairly comprehensive system of consultation for structure and local plans involving a number of stages: publicity for proposals, seeking representations, consultations, objections, and ending with a public inquiry. The main round of consultations took place in the 1970s and early 1980s.

Most major highway proposals are also examined by public inquiry. In recent years these have led to lengthy, bitter battles with objectors, and as a result, statutory procedures have been altered to make them fairer, clearer, and less capable of exploitation. According to Anthony Ramsay,

> "some local authorities (councillors and/or staff) have found their attempts to involve the public unsuccessful in attracting a meaningful proportion of the public to participate, or to be politically embarrassing. Others have deemed it unduly expensive or delaying to induce active and continuing interest on the part of the public. Such experiences have thus created a bureaucratic reaction of cynicism or great caution in some quarters. Others, however, have achieved happier outcomes and are enthusiastically developing and refining their consultative machinery".(19)

The same comments can be applied to consultation over general plans.

To help improve consultation processes, planners must accept that they are planning with people rather than for them. At its worst, the bureaucratic system of consultation ensures no more than that plans are produced, shown to the public according to the strict letter of the law, representations sought (perhaps also taken into account), and that is the end of the matter. But lay-people find it very difficult to comment on developments that have not yet taken place. It is only after the event—when they have been able to test the results—that they can formulate a view.

Successful consultation involves first, finding out what people think, what their needs are. 'If you wish to design enjoyment into a pedestrian journey', said Walsh to the Cheshire conference on road safety, "then ask the pedestrian what he thinks about it. Analyse the reaction and response from pedestrians in any pedestrian flow area to learn from their likes and dislikes of location, design, function, safety and security. Research what you have—design and implement then research again what you have provided. Any other consumer product would be treated in this way, why not pedestrian facilities? They are after all just another consumer product" (20).

Second, it is important to realise that consultation is a continuing process—a dialogue that develops on both sides because people listen to each other and respond. This is particularly important when planning for safety because perceptions can differ from facts. People's views should be sought, but they may also need explanations and education. For example, a commonsense view would suggest that crossing roads at roundabouts is more difficult and dangerous for pedestrians than crossing at traffic lights. Yet evidence has shown that precisely the opposite may be true (21).

Norman Sheppard of the Department of the Environment has made a similar point about the success of Dutch traffic schemes. 'One of the essential points about the Dutch approach', he said,

"is the intensive and extensive amount of consultation that goes on before and during design and continues to decide details on the location and type of parking, shops, access, cycle routes etc. I think this is probably one of the prime reasons for their success and acceptance. Consultation should also not stop with implementation but continue to monitor the effects of change" (22).

Councils could also experiment with non-statutory forms of consultation, for example through public representation on road safety committees.

(d) Consultation on traffic orders

Statutory procedures also require the public to be informed about individual developments—new buildings, say, or changes to existing streets such as closing roads, creating one-way streets, play streets and so on.

Concerning this last group, local authorities have statutory powers to make orders to regulate traffic, generally under the Road Traffic Regulation Act 1984 and the Heavy Commercial Vehicle (Controls and Regulations) Act 1973. The Secretary of State has reserve powers, and some orders require ministerial consent, such as reducing speed limits to below 30 mph.

Before making the orders, the local authority must usually consult the chief police officer, the highway authority, any relevant Crown authority, and organisations representing people using the road or likely to be affected by the order. Then they must publish notice of proposals in a local newspaper, the *London Gazette*, and on site.

Any objections to the order must be made within 28 or 21 days, depending on the type of order. Public inquiries may be held and must in certain circumstances—for example, when objections are made to orders prohibiting loading or unloading or by public transport operators about the creation of one-way streets. Where ministerial consent is needed for an order, the Secretary of State may require an inquiry to be held before he reaches a decision.

Statutes dictate the contents of the notices, and as a result local newspapers are filled with pages of identical advertisements written in technical jargon. They are boring, repetitive, inaccessible, and virtually unreadable. To make this kind of consultation effective, notices need to be redesigned and written in plain English. If their intention is to inform people about the nature and effect of orders, and to seek their reasoned objections, people must be encouraged to read the orders in the first place.

Some specific issues

We now turn to some specific issues concerned with planning for new sites, planning for existing sites including pedestrianisation, and planning for people with mobility handicaps, including pavement design.

(a) Planning for new sites

Planning trends go in waves, as each new generation of planners invents its own solutions. The problems of pedestrians can largely be attributed to conflict with cars. In the 1950s and early 1960s, the favoured solution to this conflict was to segregate different forms of traffic. Housing estates sprang up with separate walkways for pedestrians. Many of the new towns, too, were designed on the principle of segregation. Stevenage, for example, was the first town to have a wholly pedestrianised centre for shopping and business, with the town centre linked to the adjoining areas by underpasses or bridges across the main roads. Away from the town centre, there is an extensive system of footways segregated from road traffic and sharing underpasses with a cycleway network.

The trouble was that although these new towns and estates might have achieved a better accident record, the separate walkways were not always popular with pedestrians who felt more vulnerable to personal attack. And areas devoted solely to pedestrians can be rather bleak. Redditch Borough Council—which supports the principle of segregation developed by its predecessor Development Corporation—pointed out to us that, to be succcessful, major footpath routes must have a strong individual identity; and that even with separate facilities 'some pedestrians still walk on carriageways'(23).

Raised walkways on large estates have been one of the factors associated with problems of 'crime, vandalism, graffiti and fear of crime'. In the case of one 'problem estate' in London, overhead walkways have been described as 'The greatest single detrimental design factor' which '....plainly contribute to all three major problems on the estate (anonymity, lack of surveillance, and proliferation of escape routes'(24).

Now the planning pendulum is swinging the other way towards shared use facilities on the Dutch 'woonerf' principle. Instead of creating separate pavements for people and roads for vehicles, the carriageway is open to all forms of traffic, including people, but design features like bends, bollards, road humps, reduced visibility and so on aim to reduce vehicle speeds so that pedestrians have priority.

"A 'woonerf' is an area in which the residential functions clearly predominate over any provision for traffic. It does not mean an area free of traffic or cars, for in principal all vehicles are allowed admittance" but "the design and layout... must express the fact that traffic is subordinate to pedestrians."(25)

But novel designs also raise problems of public acceptance. A survey of safety on innovative estates, reported in the *Architects Journal,* pointed out that although the design features successfully altered drivers' behaviour, making them aware that pedestrians had priority, pedestrians did not always share this confidence.

"Asked whether they considered safety to be a problem, overall 56 per cent of residents of innovative estates said yes. The main reasons given for lack of safety were the absence of footpaths beside roads, cars speeding and problems of visibility. Although some of the comments were objective observations such as a lack of footpaths or children playing on roads, these observations on safety largely anticipated possible accidents." (26)

In other words, the estates were safer than people felt them to be. On some estates in Birmingham, a drainage channel in the carriageway delineating a nominal footway made people feel safer, perhaps because it marked a return to a more traditional street layout.

The implication is that planners must be flexible in their approach, recognising that people might not always like their perfectly logical solutions. Consultation is the key, combined with a certain humility, or at least a hesitation about imposing untested solutions on people who will have to live with them. As Walsh made clear:

> "The success of traffic restraints and pedestrian facilities in creating a more liveable environment requires bold and innovative approaches, careful planning co-operation with residents, developers and public officials and most of all a willingness to experiment in trying new ideas but it is quite clear that the implementation of the woonerf principles can be studied, amended and used as a design base but under no circumstances should it be considered that the Dutch concept can be translated in its total form to any other country." (27)

(b) Planning for existing sites

The range of planning options for existing sites is obviously more limited than for new ones, but a lot can be—and is being—done. Some 63 district councils in England and Wales responded to a request for information for our work circulated by the Association of District Councils. Most listed the measures they had introduced to help pedestrian movement. These included the following:

★ pedestrianisation schemes in town centres involving full or partial restriction of vehicles;
★ traffic management measures in town centres and residential areas, including the provision of off-street car parking in new developments, footways, footpaths and children's play areas;
★ measures to improve walking conditions for people with mobility handicaps, including dropped kerbs, use of new tactile surfaces, network routes for disabled people in town centres, the appointment of access officers, the preparation of design guides for disabled people, wheelchair clearways and so on;
★ the creation of pedestrian priority routes, or access routes through new developments (though one council—Ashfield—pointed out that residents do not like strangers);
★ the development of single surface streets with wall-to-wall paving;
★ pavement widening;
★ the provision of amenity routes, including riverside walks.

Yet in spite of the obvious concern for pedestrians shown by some councils, our surveys suggest that many pedestrians feel their needs are not adequately met. Why is this?

The submissions we received from district councils were perhaps as revealing about their failures as about their success. One council, for example, said: 'As you see, our policies and intentions are good, but do we achieve them? NO'.

Lack of progress was attributed to a number of causes. Some councils wanted more advice or information about pedestrian schemes. Amber Valley, for example, said there was little guidance nationally to help determine policies; and Leicester City Council—which has a good reputation for planning for pedestrians—said it would welcome information on schemes that had been successfully adopted elsewhere.

Lack of money was cited as a problem in many areas: Chiltern Borough Council said it had wanted to pedestrianise Chesham's main shopping street but had been forced to delay the project because of lack of funds. Several councils referred to reduced government funds, especially for footway maintenance.

Two district councils implicitly criticised their county council, one for providing insufficient back-up for road safety committees, and the other for blocking the district council's planned extension to pedestrianised streets. (Another pedestrianisation scheme in Hove was defeated by shopkeepers' opposition.)

Pedestrians themselves came in for some criticism. One council suggested that they must be educated to show road discipline. Another that 'walking is a significant form of transport... but the walking public are particularly lazy'. This last comment was echoed by a council which had built a number of subways: 'sadly they are not always popular because of our lazy nature or perhaps they are perceived to be dangerous areas for personal attack.'

Cherwell District Council emphatically denied our assertion that walking has been ignored. The Council listed its achievements such as pedestrian priority areas, the removal of through-traffic, restricted vehicle access, rear servicing of shops, and in new developments the provision of direct, safe and attractive walking routes, especially for children. 'The difficulty with which we are faced every day', said the Council's Chief Planning and Development Officer,' is striking the right balance between the needs of pedestrians and a host of other conflicting planning considerations.'

The creation of pedestrian zones is one issue where other interests can dominate, particularly those of shopkeepers who fear that trade will suffer. In the action guide for local groups, which we are publishing simultaneously with this report, we include a section on how local people might tackle problems caused by the volume of traffic, prepared for us by Transport and Environmental Studies (TEST). Among other things, this gives advice on how local people might press for the creation of pedestrian-only streets.

As TEST explains:

"There are in fact very few 'pedestrian-only' streets in Britain or anywhere else. They all have to be serviced, and not many can accomplish all of this from the rear of the premises. They all occasionally need to admit emergency vehicles. They normally permit some mechanised access for the acutely-disabled. In West Germany taxis and cyclists are freely admitted, at all times, in many cities.

However, the pedestrian usually predominates. Pedestrian streets take various forms. They may be built newly, as in some New Towns. They may be within enclosed shopping centres. Or, the majority form, an existing all-traffic street is converted. This action has been possible since the 1967 Road Traffic Regulation Act and the later 1971 Town & Country Planning Act.

How is it decided to convert a street primarily for walkers? Pressure from the walkers themselves is important. Shopkeepers are unlikely to ask for it unless they have seen successful schemes elsewhere for they believe, wrongly in most cases, that trade will deteriorate. Politicians may believe it is necessary both to conserve an historic part of the town and to stem outward movement, to the suburbs and beyond, of central area functions. Traffic planners are very wary for they see it as a loss of movement space. Public transport operators do not want anything to reduce their accessibility to the centre."(28)

The authors recommend that people should become informed about the sheer quantity of pedestrianisation that has taken place in Britain, Europe, North America and elsewhere, and about its normally beneficial effect on trade (29). They also suggest people should mobilise support as widely as possible, and get advice from people experienced in pedestrianisation who can think through all the aspects of the scheme.

One problem about pedestrianisation brought to our attention by York City Council is that while conditions in the pedestrian zone in the town centre might improve, traffic is displaced to surrounding areas (30). This can make pedestrian movement to and from the core more difficult, and underlines the need to consider pedestrian movement throughout a whole area. It is becoming even more of a problem in those towns which are extending their pedestrianised areas outwards from the centres, and reinforces McMillen's point that the benefits from pedestrianisation cannot be assumed: they should be quantified for each individual scheme (31).

(c) Planning for people with mobility handicaps

A large number of people in this country can be described as having a mobility handicap—perhaps as many as ten million, or just under one in five of the population (32). Guidelines produced by the Institution of Highways and Transportation (IHT) emphasise how wide the definition of 'mobility handicap' is:

> "It can be—and usually is—something as familiar as having to cope with children, shopping or luggage (with or without the aid of push-chairs and/or wheeled trolleys). It can mean the long-term and progressive problems of increasing age. It can also mean the temporary, but by no means short-term, difficulties occasioned by pregnancy, or an accident. Other mobility handicaps result from various kinds of physical, sensory and mental disabilities; these can involve a significant degree of extra effort, stress and pain in getting about, on the roads and in various modes of transport."(33)

As a general rule, the best way to provide for people with a mobility handicap is not to provide separate facilities, but to make sure that the facilities provided for all pedestrians can be used by the least mobile. This will benefit everyone.

There are, of course, technical developments aimed at people with specific disabilities. Textured paving surfaces, for example, can alert blind people to crossing points; flush kerbs help people in wheelchairs (and people with prams). The IHT guidelines are extremely useful in this respect. They cover design standards for movement, crossing facilities, parking, public transport, information and publicity, guidelines for development roads, and duties to disabled people in the execution of works.

An issue currently of concern to many disabled people is access to pedestrianised areas. The Department of Transport receives a steady influx of letters on this subject. For people with the most severe physical handicaps, private transport represents the most important aid to getting about outside the home. If this group is not to be denied the benefits of pedestrianised streets, they need access for their vehicles and/or special parking spaces within a very short distance of their destinations. Special parking spaces under the Orange Badge Scheme are usually provided, but there is a widespread (though unsubstantiated) feeling among non-disabled people that the Orange Badge Scheme is being abused.

The current Local Transport Note on the preparation of pedestrianisation schemes is about to be (December 1986) revised (34). Greater emphasis will be placed on consultation with disabled people.

Finally we turn to some developments in pavement design which could be particularly useful to people with mobility handicaps.

We have already seen how, in some new residential estates and existing environmental areas, pavements are disappearing completely and the roadway released to all kinds of traffic, including pedestrians. An opposite approach is to design pavements so that pedestrians clearly have priority.

One way to do this is to have raised footways across roads at pedestrian crossing points. We know of at least one council—Nottingham City Council—which is experimenting in this way (35). Carriageways have been narrowed at crossing points, and a plateau or causeway constructed across the road, ramped on either side, at the same level and in the same materials as the footway. 'The whole purpose of this work', Nottingham's Director of Technical Services told us, 'is to improve conditions for pedestrians, giving them priority when crossing roads.'

Another way of making plain that pavements are for people, described as the Magic Carpet Approach, was put forward by the Causey Campaign in Sheffield (36). The campaign recommended that part of each pavement should be separated off for the sole use of pedestrians and those travelling at walking pace (such as prams, wheelchairs, and children on trikes with their parents). The surface of the carpet should be level, unobstructed, and clearly distinguished through the use of a colour and tactile border, or by its being raised above other paving. Intersections at road junctions and driveways should be ramped, and the width dependent on pedestrian traffic: the minimum width should allow a pair of pedestrians to pass another pair without having to leave the carpet. 'When the approach is fully implemented,' said the Campaign, 'it should be possible for a pedestrian to walk safely and without obstruction from any part of Sheffield to any other part.'

The way forward

Our discussion of planning for pedestrians has suggested some improvements to the way plans are produced at the local authority level. The collection of information about pedestrian needs, the preparation of pedestrian movement plans and pedestrian impact statements—and the continual review of these plans—should help to lift pedestrians from their status near the bottom of the planning pile. Better public consultation should encourage a dialogue between the public and the council, both professionals and politicians.

Central government must also take the lead to ensure that pedestrians get a fair deal from the land use and transport planning systems. Transport Minister, Peter Bottomley has claimed that pedestrians have become the Cinderellas of road users. One-third of all journeys are made on foot and most other trips also include some walking. 'That makes pedestrians the most important class of road user. Too often planners seem to forget that' (37).

His words should lead to action. At the very least government must make sure that the needs of pedestrians are properly considered in transport policies and programmes, and structure/local plans, and that funds are available to make this practicable.

In June 1980 the then Transport Minister announced that the government would issue a green paper on walking. Two years later no such review had occurred and the government formally confirmed that it felt this to be no longer appropriate. Given the stated commitment of the present Transport Minister, Peter Bottomley, to pedestrians' interests, the time would now seem right for the government to review its intentions.

References to chapter 6

1. A. Hitchcock and C.G.B. Mitchell, 'Man and his transport behaviour. Part 2a Walking as a means of transport', *Transport Reviews*, 1984, vol.4, no.2, pp.177-187.
2. S. Potter, *Modal conflict at the mezzo-scale*, Open University New Towns Study Unit, 1978.
3. O. Lovemark, *New approaches to pedestrian problems: duplications from study of pedestrian behaviour. Transport systems for major activity centres*, OECD, Paris, 1970.
4. Market & Opinion Research International, *Pedestrians*, summary report prepared for National Consumer Council, MORI, February 1986.
5. S.W. Town, *The social distribution of mobility and travel patterns*, TRRL Laboratory Report 948, Transport and Road Research Laboratory, 1980.
6. Market Behaviour Ltd, *Inner city shopping, a qualitative study of the shopping needs of inner city consumers*, prepared for the National Consumer Council, MBL, January 1983.
7. See, for example D. Appleyard and M. Lintell, 'Environmental quality of city streets', *Journal of American Institute of Planners*, vol. 38, pp. 84-101, March 1972 and T.R. Lee, S.K. Tagg, D.J. Abbott, *Social severance by urban roads and motorways*, paper delivered at PATRAC symposium on Environmental Evaluation, 25 September 1975.
8. Marianne Hood, *Public local inquiry, the North Circular Road Hanger Lane to Harrow Road, proof of evidence*, Brent Federation of Tenants and Residents Associations (undated).

9. Tom Walsh, *Designing for the pedestrian journey in newly developing areas*, paper presented to conference on Providing for the Pedestrian, Cheshire County Council, 22 April 1986.

10. A. Hitchcock and C.G.B Mitchell, *op.cit.*

11. James Brass, Director of Planning, *Derby City Council, city centre local plan, written statement*, Derby City Council, July 1984.

12. Oxford City Council, *Oxford local plan*, Oxford City Council, March 1986.

13. A. Hitchcock and C.G.B Mitchell, *op.cit.*

14. Alan McMillen, 'Pedestrian movement in a local plan', *The Planner*, pp.20-22, January 1976.

15. Correspondence with City Planning Officer, City of York, 8 April 1986.

16. Alan McMillen, *op cit.*

17. Tom Walsh, *op.cit.*

18. Association of London Borough Engineers and Surveyors and Department of Transport, *Highways and traffic management in London: a code of practice*, HMSO, 1986.

19. Anthony Ramsay, Provision for pedestrians: the administrative context, prepared for the National Consumer Council, February 1986.

20. Tom Walsh, *op.cit.*

21. See, for example F. Webster and R. Newby, Research into the relative merits of roundabouts and traffic-signal-controlled intersections, *Proceedings of the Institution of Civil Engineers*, vol.27, p.47, 1964.

22. Norman Sheppard, *Urban areas*, paper presented to Cheshire road safety conference, see reference 9.

23. Correspondence from Chief Technical Officer, Borough of Redditch, 6 and 14 March 1986.

24. Peter Walters, 'The Mozart Estate, City of Westminster', *Housing Review*, vol.35, no. 5, September-October 1986.

25. Royal Dutch Touring Club and Ministry of Transport and Public Works, *Woonerf*, The Hague,1980.

26. Michael Jenks, 'Are innovative estates safer?' *Architects' Journal*, 29 June 1983.

27. Tom Walsh, *op.cit.*

28. Teresa Ryszkowska, Jonathan Wade and John Roberts, *Solutions to problems of pedestrians crossing roads*, a report by TEST for NCC, July 1986.

29. See, for example, Robert Brambilla et al, *American urban malls: a compendium*, US Department of Housing and Development, 1977; Rolf Monheim, *Fussgangerbereiche*, Koln, Deutscher Stadtetag,

1975; and John Roberts, *Pedestrian precincts in Britain*, London Transport and Environment Studies, 1981.

30. See reference 15 above.
31. Alan McMillen, *op.cit.*
32. Institution of Highways and Transportation, *Guidelines for providing for people with a mobility handicap*, IHT, February 1986.
33. Ibid.
34. *Notes on the preparation of pedestrianisation schemes*, Local Transport Note 2:78, Department of Transport, Welsh Office.
35. Correspondence from John Haslam, Director of Technical Services, City of Nottingham, 16 April 1986.
36. John Mitchell, *The Causey Campaign, report by working party*, Sheffield Branch of National Federation (UK) of the Blind, July 1985.
37. 'Fairer deal urged for pedestrians', *Daily Telegraph*, 28 April 1986.

Chapter 7
Pedestrian injury and death: a modern epidemic

Historically, road vehicle accidents involving pedestrians increased throughout the century up until the middle of the 1960s. Pedestrian fatalities reached their peak in 1966, when 3,153 were killed, and then began gradually to decline. In 1985, 1,789 pedestrians died in motor accidents on Britain's roads (1). While this is the lowest figure for deaths since records began in 1927, it remains the highest single category of road-user deaths, and accounts for almost a third of the total. A further 61,390 pedestrians were recorded as injured, though this figure is thought, even by government officials, to be on the low

Table 7.1 Pedestrian deaths per 100,000 population, international comparisons

Netherlands	1.5
Sweden	1.8
Denmark	2.5
Norway	2.7
Italy	2.7
Japan	2.8
USA	3.0
Finland	3.0
German Democratic Republic	3.3
Great Britain	3.4
Belgium	3.4
Spain	3.5
France	3.5
Federal Republic of Germany	3.7
Northern Ireland	4.1
Czechoslovakia	4.2
Greece	4.9
Hungary	5.4
Poland	6.0

Source: Table 47, *Road Accidents Great Britain*, 1985.

side when compared with hospital records. It may underestimate the true position by 20 per cent for serious and 40 per cent for slight injuries (2).

Table 7.1 compares the number of pedestrians killed on the roads in different countries. Great Britain appears almost exactly in the middle of the table though, compared with countries that have similar populations, road networks and traffic (Netherlands and Japan), rates poorly. Britain compares particularly badly with these two countries in terms of pedestrian accidents involving the under-25s (3).

People at risk

(a) The most vulnerable

Some groups of pedestrians are far more vulnerable than others.

Children are the first 'at risk' group: more than half of all pedestrian casualties in 1985 were under the age of nineteen. While the statistics point to a decline in accidents for younger children, the trend is upwards for the 10-14 and 15-19 age groups. The 10-14 year olds are particularly vulnerable, accounting for 10,845 deaths and injuries in 1985. ·

The elderly are a second 'at risk' group, whose likelihood of being killed is especially high. Over one-third of pedestrian deaths in 1984 were among the over-70s.

Men are more vulnerable than women: for all ages, the casualty rates are substantially higher than for women.

(b) Where and when?

Overwhelmingly, pedestrian accidents happen in built-up areas (95 per cent of casualties). Perhaps not surprisingly, the main 'conflict' points— where people meet vehicles—are also the main sites for accidents: in 1984 over half of all casualties were at *junctions*; whilst 21 per cent of adults and 13 per cent of children killed or injured were on or near a *pedestrian crossing* (4).

Some 60 per cent of the accidents involving children happened within a quarter of a mile of their own home, frequently as a result of a child being masked from the driver's view by stationary vehicles (nearly a third of the under-15s were hurt in this way (5)).

(c) Exposure to danger

Official accident records do not give the whole picture of the danger of walking because people's walking habits vary (please see Appendix B, Who Walks Where?). If accident statistics were related to the amount of walking done by different groups in different situations, we would have a much clearer idea of the risk to individuals of having an accident.

We know, for example, from the few available studies (6) that women walk approximately one-third more than men, yet both boys and men are more likely to have accidents.

For each journey made on foot, the under-14s are three times more likely to be injured than adults. The risk to the elderly is similarly heightened when account is taken of the relatively short journeys they make.

It seems that the risk to all pedestrians of dying in an accident is higher at night, and especially on Friday nights.

(d) Pedestrians' views: danger

A survey published in 1980 by the Office of Population Censuses and Surveys (OPCS) sought people's views on road safety (7). Respondents were asked to name the kinds of things which they thought made the roads in general dangerous for pedestrians. They were then asked to think of one particular location which they considered a danger spot. The five top responses were:

	Roads in general %	Particular danger spot %
Parked vehicles	17	11
Speed of traffic	17	26
Lack of pedestrian facilities	15	24
Volume of traffic	11	28
Junctions	5	33

OPCS found that 57 per cent of their sample considered road-crossing to be more difficult than five years previously. Overwhelmingly, this was blamed on increased volumes of traffic (89 per cent) and faster traffic (28 per cent).

Traffic speed again featured when informants were asked to name the things that drivers did which annoyed pedestrians. Twenty-two per cent mentioned 'driving too fast'—the second most frequent complaint after 'do not give way at crossings' (39 per cent).

A concern with traffic and road crossing featured significantly in our own survey (see chapter 2 and Table 7.2)

Table 7.2 Top five main problems for pedestrians in their own area

Problem	Spontaneous responses	Total, spontaneous and prompted responses
	%	%
Too much traffic/busy roads	22	37
Cracks or uneven pavements	19	46
No pedestrian crossings	11	23
Dog dirt on pavements	8	42
Vehicles parked on pavements	7	24

(Base: 2034)

Source: Market & Opinion Research International, *Pedestrians*, report for the National Consumer Council, Table 4a/b, MORI, February 1986.

In total, 14 per cent of survey respondents declared pedestrian conditions to be 'unsafe' to a degree.

(e) Pedestrians' views: accidents

In the OPCS survey 3 per cent of people said they had been knocked down by a vehicle during their adult life, and another 33 per cent could recall having had a near accident.

OPCS also probed respondents about the circumstances of their accident or near-miss:

Crossing at pedestrian crossing, vehicle ignoring crossing 17%
Crossing without looking, vehicle travelling along the road 11%
Crossing the road, vehicle travelling too fast 11%
Crossing the road, vehicle turning a corner 11%

Our own survey revealed that 2 per cent of adults had been involved in vehicle or motorcycle accidents as pedestrians in the previous year (8). In line with the national picture, men were more frequently involved, accounting for 59 per cent of accidents involving cars.

Consumer principles on road safety

Pedestrians should be able to make their journeys without risk to life and limb. More than this, they should—ideally—not suffer restrictions on their movement or convenience as a price of improved safety.

In reality public highways are provided for many uses and kinds of transport, not just walking. So some compromise is inevitable between the conflicting priorities of different road-users. At minimum, however, pedestrians should expect to receive parity of treatment with other road-users in terms of provision for their needs and regard for their safety on the roads.

Such a statement is modest enough: it accepts *some* element of inconvenience or delay in order to accommodate the safety requirements of others. It also indicates our belief that the current balance of provision is biased against people travelling on foot. An effective redress of this bias will inevitably be at the expense of the *convenience* of other road-users, although *not* their safety.

Road safety measures

There are three main types of measures that can make the roads safer for road-users in general, and pedestrians in particular:

★ *education and publicity* to highlight dangers and encourage 'safe' habits and behaviour;

★ *enforcement of the law* on road offences to ensure that the rights and responsibilities of different road users are observed;

★ *engineering and traffic management* measures to reduce the number or severity of conflict points between different types of road users.

(a) Education and publicity

The promotion of road safety—through advertising, information, propaganda or campaign materials—and more formal and systematic education, is a major plank of national and local government measures. In addition to the Department of Transport's own national publicity campaigns, the Royal Society for the Prevention of Accidents (RoSPA) undertakes publicity and education development work; and local authority road safety officers co-ordinate local initiatives, under the legal duty placed on councils in England and Wales since 1974 to promote road safety.

The block Treasury allocations for road safety publicity remain fairly static in real terms, according to the Department of Transport, but the budget is sometimes topped-up from within the Department. So in the financial year 1983/84, a total of approximately £5.5 million on publicity included £2 million on a pedestrian safety campaign, mainly TV advertising. In 1984/85 the overall total dropped to £4.2 million, with

£1.1 million on pedestrians. In the 1986/87 financial year, the aim is to promote longer-lasting safety awareness by all road-users, and the more continuous promotion has excluded the use of the expensive TV campaign.

Publicity and education are mainly targeted at the most accident-prone categories of road-user, so children and the elderly feature as the focus of many of these initiatives. The traditional message to pedestrians has been very much one of modifying their behaviour to avoid clashing with traffic. For children this has meant learning the advice of the Green Cross Code, a formal set of instructions for safe road crossing. Talks, films, leaflets, posters, information manuals, radio and TV advertising are all included in the repertory of road safety promotion for pedestrians. It is very difficult to measure the effectiveness of road safety campaigns, and the Department of Transport's review of road safety publicity is ambivalent in its assessment of the success of its own campaigns. A report published in 1978 by OECD estimated that a publicity campaign combined with the Green Cross Code helped in an 11 per cent reduction in casualties.

The government's Transport and Road Research Laboratory (TRRL) is currently funding research into a major review of road safety education. Early results confirm that 63 per cent of schools have no structured road safety teaching programme (9). Most schools rely on talks in assembly or occasional visits by outsiders to get the message across. Dr Amarjit Singh concluded from these survey findings that 'traffic safety is not considered a priority subject' and 'This lack of priority may be a major reason for traffic safety education's present fragmented and inconsistent implementation in British primary and middle schools'(10).

An initiative by the Greater London Council drew upon Scandinavian experience of pre-school Traffic Clubs, where a 40 per cent reduction in accident involvement is claimed for those children taking part. In March 1985, the GLC set up the 'Streetwise Kids' Traffic Club, which involved direct-mailing road safety booklets to parents at six-monthly intervals to help them build up a progressive programme with their child(ren) in the home, through games and exercises which have been devised by TRRL. The scheme is so far unique in this country, with approximately 25,000 children participating. It is currently being funded by the London boroughs following GLC abolition. Although arrangements are being made for monitoring and evaluation, it is thought to be too early to assess its impact properly, though the Department of Transport is watching its progress and actively considering a similar scheme on a national basis.

At the other end of the range of vulnerable pedestrians, Southampton

University's Health Education Unit, under contract to TRRL, has undertaken a three-year study into ways of improving communication of road safety advice to the elderly. This will take account of the practical difficulties of reaching the target group since, unlike children, they have no guaranteed or regular meeting points at which advice can be easily disseminated.

Education and publicity programmes seem to be weakest in their coverage of the 10-19 age group, where accidents are on the increase. Within this age range the transition from child to adult road-crossing behaviour takes place.

Education and publicity tend to concentrate on increasing the *pedestrian's* awareness of unsafe road conditions, and the need to guard against bad driver behaviour. Perhaps insufficient effort is put into emphasising the responsibilities and role of drivers in accident prevention. For example, the official Department of Transport *Manual for Drivers* (a reference work widely used by driving instructors) among thirty pages of detailed explanation and advice on driver conduct at junctions, devotes only five lines of comment specifically to pedestrians. Yet 59 per cent of pedestrian casualties on built-up roads happen at junctions. The section on children omits any reference to the hazard of parked cars masking a child, although this factor features in nearly one-third of injuries to children under fifteen. Education on pedestrian safety should be seen as a matter for drivers, not primarily for pedestrians. It should be given a more prominent place in all driver training material, and in the driving test, to examine drivers' awareness and ability to handle the major road situations likely to cause accidents to pedestrians.

(b) Law and enforcement

There is a substantial body of law relating to the rights, restrictions and duties of road traffic. Much of it relates *indirectly* to road safety, but very little is laid down by statute on pedestrians' rights in relation to other road-users. ˙

The absence of a legal framework correspondingly implies an absence of *restrictions* on pedestrians, so for example, they have a common law right to walk on the highway, except motorways, providing they take reasonable care, and may generally cross the road wherever they want to.

The most significant legal right of pedestrians is in respect of pedestrian crossings. At zebra crossings pedestrians have precedence over vehicles once they have stepped onto the crossing, and at pelicans pedestrians have right of way so long as they are not crossing on the red signal.

Pedestrian behaviour in relation to other road-users is laid out in more detail in the *Highway Code*, the well-known title of the detailed instructions for the guidance of road-users issued by the Secretary of State under section 37 of the Road Traffic Act 1972 (as substituted by the Transport Act 1982, section 60). The code itself is not a legally-binding document, but adherence to its advice *is* taken into account in court cases involving road accidents.

One way of trying to improve road safety through changes in the law would be to increase the legal constraints on pedestrians. However, given the near-impossibility of controlling pedestrian behaviour it seems unlikely that this approach would be very successful. In the early 1960s there were a couple of experiments in London using red line road markings designed to confine road-crossing to specific points. Crossing the red lines was made an offence. These early brushes with 'jaywalking' legislation were universally considered to have failed, and were never taken any further. They would, in any case, be unwelcome, because further restrictions would almost certainly increase the inconvenience of walking journeys, and therefore worsen existing inequalities.

An alternative approach, advocated widely by road safety and environmental groups, is to increase the restrictions on other road users, both to increase the sanctions against bad driving, and to encourage good driving. Suggestions range from the compulsory fitting of 'speed-alerting devices' in all cars to alert the driver, other road users and the police that the speed limit was being exceeded; through random breath-testing for drunk-driving to harsher penalities for all forms of driving offence.

We have seen that vehicle speed is a major source of pedestrian complaint, and there is now substantial international agreement and evidence on the positive correlation between higher vehicle speed, accident frequency and severity of injuries (11). Britain has higher speed limits than some other countries (such as the USA, New Zealand and Scandinavia).

But the Department of Transport sees the problem as having less to do with formal speed limits than with *actual* speeds and thus, drivers' perceptions of the appropriate speed for the particular road and conditions at the time. The most effective way of altering perceptions, they argue, is through changes to the physical environment rather than legislative control. We return to this in the section on traffic management below. However, it is well evidenced that enforcement (or threat of it) does affect both speed and accident rates. It is also believed to be deeply unpopular with motorists, though there is little formal evidence to support this view. The dilemma was summarised by the Parliamentary Advisory Council on Transport and Safety (PACTS):

"There is clear evidence that if sufficient police enforcement is applied, dramatic improvements can be achieved by way of reductions in vehicle speeds and accidents. There is also evidence that, in spite of publicly expressed concern about road accidents, drivers are not prepared to moderate their speeds to conform with the law and with safety requirements generally unless forced to do so for fear of police action. The police, themselves, are reluctant to increase enforcement either by conventional means or by improved technology for fear of losing public co-operation and prefer methods which do not require direct police action."(12)

We would suggest, then, that a major burden of responsibility here must rest with the police either to risk some unpopularity or actively to promote indirect enforcement techniques.

Another area where the low risk of detection seems to encourage offenders is drunk-driving. The chances of being caught have been estimated at only one in 250 (13). Pedestrian drunkenness is also a significant factor in road accidents. In 28 per cent of pedestrian deaths during 1984, blood alcohol levels exceeded the drivers' legal maximum, rising to two-thirds of those killed between 10pm and 4am (14). This is a cause for concern, though it should be noted that drunken pedestrians put their own safety, rather than the safety of others, at risk.

As we write, the penalties for driving offences are the subject of a major review of road traffic law (the 'North Review'), due to report its findings in the spring of 1987. In general terms we are sceptical that the present tendency to regard offences such as parking, careless driving and the contravention of pedestrian crossing regulations as relatively 'minor', can do very much to encourage good driving behaviour.

However, tighter legislative controls and tougher penalties can only be effective if law enforcement is adequate. In our discussions with both the Metropolitan Police and the Association of Chief Police Officers (ACPO), the police felt that higher priority should be given to traffic matters generally, but that in competition with other demands on police time, traffic and road safety feature rather low down the list. Clearly, if a greater priority is to be given to the enforcement of traffic offences, the level of resources allocated to it must be reviewed. The police argue that it is a lack of manpower, as well as the need to 'police by consent', that determines the level of enforcement. We hope that the extension of fixed penalty fines to a range of motoring offences will aid the more vigorous enforcement of the law.

Lack of sufficient enforcement seems particularly acute in two matters that affect pedestrian safety: speeding and parking. Positive measures to change drivers' attitudes might include:

★ consideration of a 'probationary year' for new drivers (a practice in some other countries), during which conviction for *any* driving offence would require retraining and possibly retesting. Evidence suggests that new drivers are particularly accident-prone; and such a measure could help instil longer-term good driving;

★ the adoption by police of various devices (including dummy patrol cars, cameras at traffic lights and radar warning notices) which might act as deterrents to illegal driving.

(c) Traffic management/engineering measures

Increasingly, those concerned with road safety and the interests of pedestrians have been looking at ways of altering the built environment to influence the behaviour of road-users. It is fairly clear that long, wide, well-surfaced, straight roads are incentives to faster driving, whereas the introduction of landscaping features (trees, shrubs, bends and curves) or physical characteristics (road markings, road narrowing, rumble-strips, humps, etc.) will tend to make traffic proceed more cautiously. Physical measures are also used to control *pedestrian* behaviour, for instance by providing railings to stop people crossing the road in the vicinity of a pedestrian crossing.

Physical measures embrace a huge range of possibilities, from major planning and redevelopment schemes (bypasses, city-centre pedestrianisation) to small, cheap, one-off features (such as a refuge or island in the middle of a road). The type of measures that can be used, and the ways that they are used, will also depend greatly on the type of area.

Existing urban centres: over the past fifteen years many of Britain's existing town centres have been extensively redeveloped to exclude most vehicles from major shopping areas. Pedestrian precincts have become a standard feature, and numerous councils are now embarking on 'phase two' redevelopments to extend pedestrianised areas outwards from the town centre. Even in those towns where full-scale pedestrianisation is impracticable, the visitor will expect to find one or two central streets with very limited vehicle access. In road safety terms, individual pedestrian precincts have produced lower accident rates, but no major recent study has been done on the national picture. It is possible that the displacement of vehicles to roads around the centre of towns has the effect of making those roads more dangerous for pedestrians.

Pedestrianisation is a large-scale and long-term initiative and, of course, expensive. Other smaller and more isolated traffic management measures are also common in urban centres, including one-way systems, restrictions on types of vehicles using certain roads, or banning turning by traffic at specific times of the day.

Existing residential areas: it is in local streets and estates that road safety initiatives are least-developed, and yet most acutely needed, particularly for child safety. Where street networks are well-established, the scope for major redesign or engineering work is limited. This is where a combination of traffic management—forcing cars onto the main feeder (distributor) roads and away from the local back streets—and small-scale physical measures can be most appropriate. A major European review of road safety measures in 1979 (15) suggested that measures in traditional residential areas should aim to:

a. discourage or prevent non-access traffic using residential access streets and local distributors, and

b. promote satisfactory standards of behaviour in those drivers for whom access to such streets is justified.

New urban developments have tended to aim for *segregation* of pedestrian and vehicular traffic. In some instances, such as Stevenage and Harlow, extensive cycle and pedestrian networks have been developed. Their design has tried to minimise inconvenience so as to encourage full use. The safety record of the new towns is considerably better than that of the old urban layout; one official estimate is of an accident rate 15 per cent less than traditional areas (16).

New residential areas: new estates offer the opportunity for incorporating road safety provision from the design stage. Much experimentation has been done to improve safety features so that they are appropriate to residents' needs, do not create extra hazards, and are environmentally attractive. Road safety principles are set down for the road planners in an official Department of Environment design bulletin (17). In a summary of main objectives this bulletin states: 'Residential roads and footpaths are an integral part of housing layout where surroundings free from traffic nuisance are of prime importance; and where in the patterns of movement around buildings the needs of pedestrians for safety and convenience should be given priority in design over the use of vehicles.' Detailed attention is then given to all aspects of design features and aids, landscaping, road surface treatment, needs of cyclists, pedestrians, the elderly and disabled. This bulletin is being updated by way of a supplement, which will give greater emphasis to keeping roads short as an aid to speed reduction, and further advice on 'shared surfaces' (where vehicles and pedestrians are not divided by a proper pavement, but the road is designed to keep car speeds very low and give pedestrians priority).

It seems likely that future residential road design will favour integration rather than separation. The impact on pedestrian safety is not likely to be great, however, as the majority of accidents happen on through roads, rather than the limited range of residential streets to which these schemes can be applied.

There is no shortage of available engineering and traffic management measures already in operation in this country and abroad, which can serve substantially to improve pedestrian safety. Almost all involved in road safety policy or implementation with whom NCC spoke emphasised these kinds of measures as the way forward. Progress, however, has been slow. A number of obstacles have been identified, including:

★ Insufficient encouragement by the Department of Transport for the adoption of small-scale, low-cost measures by local authorities. It has been suggested by the Parliamentary Advisory Council on Transport Safety (PACTS) that government should monitor councils' schemes through the information it receives from transport policies and programmes submissions, and the annual transport supplementary grant (TSG) bids. PACTS has also proposed that councils be required to produce an annual report for the public on their progress in road accident remedial measures.

★ Lack of funding incentives for local authorities. Most small-scale, low-cost schemes do not qualify for financial help through the TSG system.

★ Over-restrictive regulation of certain measures, including the criteria for installing pedestrian crossings and road humps, and traffic signals with pedestrian phases. Not only is this seen to prevent local authorities meeting needs—and local people's demands—for better provision, but also to stifle experimentation and new initiatives by councils. John Brownfield, when at the GLC's Road Safety Section, argued that:
"Central government regulations, while beneficial in setting consistent standards have often been over restrictive and in some cases incorrect... in future the Department of Transport should restrict itself to setting guidelines only" (18).
This recommendation is supported by PACTS.

★ Insufficient priority given to these measures by local authorities themselves. To take just one example, of central refuges in roads, C.A. Cranley, of Essex County Council's Accident Unit comments: "whilst refuges are not a rarity there are far too few provided ... Perhaps they are regarded as obstructions to motorists, perhaps they are a maintenance liability, perhaps they are too simple and cheap to attract the attention of traffic engineers. Whatever the reason, I consider their potential unrealised" (19).

The GLC's own accident analysis on the siting of pedestrian refuges, as long ago as 1976, demonstrated a reduction in pedestrian accidents of up to 59 per cent where refuges were installed (20).

National road safety initiatives

(a) Accident blackspot

The Department of Transport's Road Safety Division is primarily responsible for initiating major new schemes on traffic safety. Over the past decade its main road engineering strategy has been the 'accident-blackspot' programme: the identification by local authorities of major casualty sites which are then treated with low-cost measures (such as traffic lights, pedestrian crossings, road markings, anti-skid road surfacing, central refuges, etc.) to reduce accident rates. The programme concentrates on eliminating the 'worst' accident clusters first. These are determined by estimating the cost of accidents minus the cost of engineering measures. The sites which produce the greatest savings are given priority, and it has been suggested that counties will normally confine their attention to schemes that produce savings of at least 50 per cent of the cost of the measures in the first year (21). It is now widely argued that this recommended rate of return is too high.

The blackspot approach has not been taken up by all local authorities. Where it has been, substantial reductions in accident rates have been claimed. However, the economic analysis through which sites are chosen makes it inevitable that, after a period of years, an authority will run out of locations which qualify for treatment.

(b) Urban safety project

As a result, the government, through TRRL, is now running a series of experiments on a new accident prevention approach designed to achieve a 15 per cent reduction in accidents. If successful, the approach might be brought into full implementation by 1995. Called the 'Urban Safety Project,' its aim is to tackle that 50 per cent of road accidents which are scattered over an area, rather than being clustered at a particular junction, bend or other identifiable blackspot. TRRL's explanatory leaflet states that:

> "Amongst these scattered accidents there is a markedly higher proportion of pedestrian and cycle accidents (especially involving children) than is found in the clusters of accidents" (22).

The strategy of the Urban Safety Project is to reshape traffic patterns by pushing cars back onto the main roads, excluding notorious 'rat-runs' through neighbourhood streets so that only access vehicles will use them, and encouraging slow and safe driving by all residential traffic. No new legal powers are envisaged: the techniques will be traffic management and engineering measures, implemented over wider areas in a planned way.

The project began in 1982 and runs for five years, including a period of evaluation, monitoring and amendment to initial schemes. Particularly welcome is its emphasis on local community consultation.

There are critics of the Projects however. Friends of the Earth suggest that they 'do nothing to improve the lot of the cyclist and pedestrian'. They also doubt that much is being done to reduce vehicle speeds in residential areas, and allege that local consultation has been minimal (23). They recommend a far greater emphasis on those measures which will force low vehicle speeds and improve environmental features, and cite a recommendation from a Parliamentary Committee in support of this emphasis:

> "The Department (of Transport) should consider setting up a demonstration project, similar in nature to the TRRL's urban safety project, which is aimed specifically at determining whether low cost engineering measures which help to reduce vehicle speeds in residential areas would significantly improve pedestrian safety (24)."

The area-wide approach may also prove less satisfactory in the busiest urban centres, where the 'main roads' (on which TRRL wants to concentrate motor traffic) are also heavily-populated residential areas.

There appears to be a shortage of research into the *circumstances* of pedestrian accidents. The absence of detailed information may lead to an undervaluing of the need for improved pedestrian provision, and is a false economy if measures *are* implemented which prove to be ineffectual. Greater attention should be given to local studies and to consultation with residents about their habits, needs and preferences. The Urban Safety Project has itself demonstrated that the introduction of such schemes also requires patience and public education. The project, like some of the novel housing estates' designs, mentioned in chapter 6, has run into problems of public acceptability.

The safety of children

Earlier in this chapter we noted the high road accident rates for children and young people.

In the neighbourhood, the two principal dangers to children at play on the street are from cars travelling too fast, and the presence of parked cars. Walsh argues that, rather than concentrating on the 'average' pedestrian, designers should provide for the most vulnerable of all: the child pedestrian (25). He recommends the creation of 50 metre street zones for children to play in, in the immediate vicinity of their homes. This is to be achieved through selective street closures, providing space for cars to turn, off-street car parking facilities (mainly for visitors rather than residents) and the introduction of engineering features to slow speed and emphasise pedestrian priority. Walsh suggests a general limit on kerbside parking for residents only and proposes that all new house plots should include parking space for two cars.

The other major source of danger is during journeys to school. Two recent developments may affect these: the deregulation of public transport and its effects on patterns, frequency and cost of public transport; and the trend of school closures and amalgamations.

The net effect of these factors, coupled with general financial stringency by local authorities, may be to increase the numbers of children having to undertake longer walking trips to school. The legal duty on local education authorities to make suitable travel arrangements for children to and from school has recently been amended, following a series of court cases. The 1944 Education Act defined a school as being within walking distance—and therefore requiring no special travel arrangements—for children under eight years living within two miles, and for children over eight living within three miles. In both cases, these distances referred to the nearest available route. The strict interpretation of the Act was challenged by the parents of a child whose direct route to school was less than three miles but was not, they claimed, 'available' as it consisted in part of an isolated, unlit track and was thus too dangerous for an unaccompanied girl to use.

In October 1986 the House of Lords rejected this argument, holding that a route did not fail to qualify as 'available' because of dangers that would only arise if a child was unaccompanied, and that the 1944 Act clearly anticipated that children would be accompanied to school (26). Following this judgement, the government inserted a new clause in the Education Bill then before parliament, requiring local education authorities to 'have regard (amongst other things) to the age of the pupil and the nature of the route, or alternatives routes, which he could reasonably be expected to take' (27). It is not yet clear what the practical effects of this will be. Clearly, the law must take account of social changes, and the safety of children travelling to school should not depend on their being accompanied. On the other hand, the amendment appears to put all the responsibilities onto the local education authority. In contrast, the Danish Road Traffic Act 1978 requirement states:

"It is the responsibility of the police and the road administration, after consultation with the schools, to make provisions for the protection of children, against the dangers of wheeled traffic, on their way to and from school (27)."

From this clear legal safety priority, the Danes have evolved a series of educational and physical measures to create safe routes to school.

These include pre-school traffic clubs, encouragement of safe cycling, and special restrictions on vehicle speeds, access and priority on the main routes used by schoolchildren. Similar programmes have been adopted in Holland and West Germany, and recent work has been done on an experimental basis in Avon, Lothian and London, by John Grimshaw Associates and Friends of the Earth to try to develop a similar approach in this country (29).

The hazard of cars collecting at school entrances was raised specifically with us by Chief Constable John Over of ACPO. Under 'Safe Routes to School' schemes, school entrances would become the centre of traffic-free blocks, mini pedestrianised zones, wherever possible, or subject to traffic management involving one-way systems and waiting and turning points, thereby reducing the danger of conflicts and accidents.

It is also claimed by C.A. Cranley (30) that schools crossing patrols (usually considered the most expensive pedestrian facility for crossing the road) are extremely effective in terms of their safety record: in Essex less than one-tenth the rate of zebra or pelican accidents.

From the available evidence it would seem that there is scope for a significant reduction in child road accidents by a combination of legal, planning and engineering measures in residential neighbourhoods and school surroundings. We urge the government, as a priority, to clarify the legal obligation on local authorities to ensure safe passage to school. Councils themselves should embark on far more radical improvements to road safety in neighbourhoods.

References to chapter 7

1. Official accident/casualty statistics quoted here and below from Department of Transport, *Road accidents Great Britain 1985*, HMSO, November 1986.
2. David Smith, *Pedestrian activity, casualties and safety, a brief introduction*, paper to Cheshire County Council conference on Providing for the Pedestrian, April, 1986.
3. Department of Transport, *op.cit.*
4. Department of Transport, *Road accidents Great Britain 1984*, Table D2, HMSO, November 1985.
5. *Ibid*, Table 31.
6. See, for example M. Hillman and A. Whalley, *Walking is transport*, Policy Studies Institute, 1979. J.E Todd and A. Walker, *People as Pedestrians*, HMSO, 1980.
7. J.E Todd and A. Walker, *op.cit.*

8. Market & Opinion Research International, *Pedestrians*, summary report prepared for the National Consumer Council, MORI, February 1986.

9. OECD report of sub-group 2: Road Safety Education, OECD 1978.

10. Amarjit Singh, 'Risks, research and resources', *Times Educational Supplement*, 30 May 1986.

11. See, for example, S. Plowden and M. Hillman, *Danger on the road: the needless scourge*, p.110, Table III.1, Policy Studies Institute, May 1984.

12. R. Newby, J. Breen, D. Gilbert, *General speed limits, a review prepared for the GLC*, PACTS, March 1986.

13. Professor R. Kendell, member of the Royal College of Psychiatrists' special committee on alcohol, quoted in the *Guardian*, 15 October 1986.

14. Department of Transport, *op.cit.*, 1986.

15. OECD Road Research Group, *Traffic safety in residential areas*, OECD, 1979.

16. David Smith, *op.cit.*

17. John Noble et al, 'Residential roads and footpaths', *Design Bulletin 32*, Department of Environment 1977.

18. John Brownfield, *Safer crossing places*, Greater London Council, March 1985.

19. C. A. Cranley, *The pedestrian within the built environment*, paper to Cheshire County Council conference on Providing for the Pedestrian, April 1986.

20. John Brownfield, *op.cit.*

21. Parliamentary Advisory Committee for Transport Safety, Evidence to House of Commons Transport Committee Inquiry into Road Safety.

22. Transport and Road Research Laboratory, *Urban safety project*, Leaflet LF938, Department of Transport, December 1982.

23. Friends of the Earth briefing paper, *Area wide road safety improvements*, FoE, February 1986.

24. Friends of the Earth briefing, House of Commons Transport Select Committee Report on Road Safety, January 1985

25. T. Walsh, *Designing for the pedestrian in newly developing areas*, paper to Cheshire County Council conference on Providing for the Pedestrian, April 1986.

26. Rodgers and another v. Essex County Council, 16 October 1986.

27. Education Bill, 1986.

28. Danish Road Traffic Act, Section 3, article 3 quoted from Don Matthew, *Safe routes to school, the European experience*, Friends of

the Earth, March 1985.

29. See John Grimshaw Associates, *Safe routes to school*, papers and final report, 1985.

30. C.A. Cranley, *op.cit.*

Chapter 8
The road to change

Until about two hundred years ago, pavements as a separate facility for pedestrians were virtually unknown and 'the highway' was intended for all types of traffic. Partly because of the slow development of the distinction between types of traffic, there is no single body of law that covers pedestrians. Nor does any one single authority—either national or local—have responsibility for pedestrian matters.

We have argued throughout this report that the pedestrian interest has suffered from this fragmentation of responsibility, partly because pedestrians, unlike other road users, have no powerful body lobbying on their behalf. In this final chapter, we consider the roles of the various authorities involved in the provision of pedestrian facilities, and bring together our specific recommendations. Local authorities figure large in our recommendations because their actions affect pedestrian interests at a number of points, not just in their role as highway authorities, but more generally in planning, creating and protecting the local environment.

Raising the status of the pedestrian

We believe that the overall status of the pedestrian has been too low, compared with other road users, and should be raised. Three broad approaches are needed: the different levels of government must set out coherent policies on their intentions for pedestrians, and ensure that their existing laws and policies are actually put into practice; sufficient funding must be provided; and more attention must be given to finding out what pedestrians want and need.

We recommend that:

8.1 *The Department of Transport should take the lead by preparing a Green Paper on walking, as originally announced in July 1980.*

8.2   The Department should investigate the possibility of establishing a national 'pedestrians week' which would, among other things, involve the police in a concerted effort to enforce those traffic offences that particularly affect pedestrians.

Responsibility for the pedestrian has to be focused, by the establishment at all levels of government, on professional groups with a remit to promote the interests of pedestrians. We therefore recommend that:

8.3   Pedestrian units should be set up within highways or transportation departments of upper-tier authorities, within district councils, spanning both engineering and planning departments, and within central government. Their brief should be to research, plan and monitor schemes designed to aid pedestrian safety, convenience and security and to improve the pleasantness of the pedestrian environment.

To ensure that the right services are provided, professionals need to ensure that pedestrians themselves are consulted:

8.4   Highways and planning authorities should undertake to collect much more information about the problems people face as pedestrians. This will help in setting priorities between different types of road user and between different pedestrian problems, and will help in predicting the demand for walking at the local level.

Of course, a great deal of good and imaginative work is already being carried out in different places around the country. It is not clear that this work is always widely known. We see a role in this for the Department of Transport, the Department of Environment, local authority associations and professional associations. We recommend that:

8.5   Formal systems should be established for the circulation and sharing of information on good practice in designing and planning for pedestrians.

We believe that there is quite widespread perception that laws designed to protect the pedestrian are weakly enforced. Local authorities, the Home Office and the police themselves all have a role to play in rectifying this. We recommend that:

8.6   The Home Office, the Department of Transport and local police committees should encourage greater priority to be given to the enforcement of road traffic law, particularly as it affects pedestrian safety.

8.7   The police should undertake a national review of ways in which they can improve the effectiveness of their role in enforcing traffic offences.

Pavement damage and maintenance

The most basic issue for pedestrians is the condition of the footway itself—its design, construction and maintenance, and indeed whether one exists at all. As we have shown, damaged pavements are the greatest single cause of dissatisfaction among pedestrians.

Footways are overwhelmingly an urban phenomenon—and particularly on unclassified roads. On average, each hundred metres of urban unclassified road has 170 metres of footway, compared with only two metres on rural unclassified roads. Of the 229,000 kilometres of total footway in England and Wales, 209,000 km (over 90 per cent) is on urban roads: indeed unclassified urban roads alone account for about 70 per cent. Only two per cent of all footways are on trunk roads (1).

Responsibility for the repair and maintenance of roads and pavements rests with the relevant highway authority. In the case of trunk roads and most motorways the Secretary of State for Transport has responsibility. For most others it is a local authority. This, depending on the road in question, includes county councils, regional councils, island councils, metropolitan districts, or London boroughs.

To complicate matters further, the actual maintenance work is not always carried out by the body that has legal responsibility for it. In London, for example, maintenance has been carried out by the boroughs, even in the case of roads that have been the responsibility of the Department of Transport or the Greater London Council. Elsewhere, the position is even more complicated, with county councils sometimes carrying out work as 'agent authorities' for the DTp on trunk roads, and sometimes delegating their own road maintenance to district councils under agency agreements. District councils can also claim the right to maintain unclassified roads and footways.

This administrative fragmentation gives rise to two sorts of problems for consumers. First, it is extremely confusing when trying to work out who is responsible for a particular pavement, making it more difficult for an individual to complain about poor conditions, say, or claim compensation for injury and damage.

It may also, in some areas at least, act against the pedestrian in the sharing out of resources for highway maintenance. Pavements are essentially of local concern, yet ultimate authority for their maintenance—and for bidding for the money for their maintenance—rests with the upper tier authorities. Even where agency agreements exist, district councils must work to broad policy and expenditure guidelines provided by the highway authority. We have argued throughout this report that, as a generalisation, highway authorities have tended to attach more importance to roads and vehicles than to the short, local journeys people make on foot.

There might therefore be a case, in principle, for locating responsibility for pedestrian facilities at the lower tier of administration—'nearer to the ground'. However, the provision and maintenance of footways is inseparable from the provision and maintenance of highways, and we do not suggest a redistribution of responsibility.

We do see the need for constant pressure to be applied on highway authorities, both upwards from the public via district councillors and downwards from central government, to ensure that pedestrians get a fairer share of available resources.

(a) Standards

Despite recent attempts to arrive at generally agreed codes of practice, it appears that the accepted standard for footway repair is likely to vary from area to area. We would suggest that there is an urgent need to establish more precise criteria for footway maintenance. This could be done by the Standing Committee on Highway Maintenance, the local authority associations, and the professional associations. We recommend that:

8.8 *New national standards should be established for footways, based on the objectives set out by the Institution of Highways and Transportation and the Association of London Boroughs Engineers and Surveyors (2).*

8.9 *Standard footway maintenance procedures should be agreed, based on the local authority associations' code of practice.*

8.10 *The standards for assessing footway deterioration in the national Road Maintenance Conditions Survey should be reviewed and tightened up, using similar standards to those in the code of practice.*

(b) Natural deterioration

The level of dissatisfaction that our surveys have revealed leads us to conclude that spending on footways needs to be increased. The overall level of funding for highway maintenance has for some time been a subject of controversy. In the case of spending on footway maintenance we believe that the problem arises from a long-term underestimate of the standards that pedestrians expect, rather than from a decline in funding levels. We would therefore argue specifically that:

8.11 *Local authorities should allocate a greater proportion of their highway budgets to improving footways.*

However, we recognise that local authorities are not free simply to determine their own levels of expenditure, and a national review of spending on footways is urgently required. The House of Commons Select Committee on Transport has carried out several reviews of highway maintenance in the past few years. We would now recommend that:

8.12 *The House of Commons Select Committee on Transport should examine the national provision for spending on footway maintenance and repair.*

To help assess priorities, we recommend that:

8.13 *The Department of Transport should produce clearer information on comparative unit costs for footway maintenance spending by each local authority and also on the total footway stock in each area.*

The starting point for any maintenance programme must clearly be the establishment of inspection procedures. Some authorities do not employ highway inspectors, apparently on the grounds that they cannot afford to. We believe that it is quite unacceptable to allow the footway to deteriorate to a point where it is dangerous to pedestrians. There would seem to be room for local authorities to extend their formal inspection system by encouraging members of the public, and indeed members of their own staff, to report footway defects, though this is no substitute for a full time professional staff. We recommend that:

8.14 *All local authorities should carry out continuous surveys to establish the level and distribution of pavement accidents in their locality, and to help set priorities for footway maintenance and repair programmes.*

8.15 *Local authorities should explore ways of involving more of their outdoor staff in the reporting of footway defects.*

8.16 *Local authorities should produce public information on the division of responsibilities for maintenance and repair of footway defects, together with contact telephone numbers and names of relevant officials.*

8.17 *Local authorities should set up straightforward procedures to allow members of the public to report pavement problems via postcard schemes, a central complaints office, etc.*

8.18 *Local authorities should keep records of all defects reported by members of the public or from other sources, and monitor the progress of repair jobs arising from these reports.*

8.19 *Local authorities should set explicit target standards of service for responding to public reports of pavement problems, including acknowledgement of the report and further communication to indicate the outcome.*

(c) Public utilities street works

Damage to pavements caused by public utilities demonstrates how a confusion of responsibilities acts against the interests of pedestrians. Despite a series of attempts over the years to co-ordinate the activities of the various parties, the Horne report showed how weak the existing agreements are. The failure to co-ordinate affects both relationships between utilities and local authorities—for example when a utility breaks up the road under 'emergency' provisions without notifying the authority—and between utilities themselves—as when a permanent restoration is made by one utility, only to be broken up again within a few weeks by another utility. We welcome the government's decision to accept the recommendations of the Horne Committee. These require legislation to bring them into force. We recommend that:

8.20 The Department of Transport should introduce legislation as soon as possible to give effect to the main recommendations of the Horne Report.

In the meantime, highway authorities should take a more robust line with the utilities, to ensure that works are notified and that repairs are carried out to a satisfactory standard as soon as possible. The highway authorities should use all legal powers at their disposal to ensure that utilities carry out adequate restoration. To encourage the co-ordination of responsibilities, and also to protect the interests of pedestrians who do suffer injury as a result of streetworks, we recommend that:

8.21 Local authorities should take responsibility for forwarding claims involving third parties (eg. utilities) to the appropriate person in those organisations, and for informing the claimant of where and why they have forwarded the claim.

(d) Pavement parking

Pavement parking is a direct source of danger and inconvenience to pedestrians, as well as being a significant cause of pavement damage. Action is urgently needed. Three approaches can be used: engineering methods, for example the use of bollards to make pavement parking physically impossible; education, for example the use of intensive publicity by the GLC, or the distribution of warning leaflets by police and others; and enforcement. Each of these approaches requires action by a number of different bodies—the local authorities, central government, the police and magistrates. We recommend that:

8.22 Local authorities should make greater efforts to introduce physical enforcement measures to prevent over-riding and parking on footways.

8.23 The Department of Transport and the Home Office should act to bring into force the provisions of the 1974 Road Traffic Act, making pavement parking illegal.

8.24 Local authorities should adopt the full range of legal powers available to deal with all pavement obstructions, particularly pavement parking. This may include the designation of council staff to carry out monitoring and enforcement duties.

8.25 The police should give higher priority to enforcing the law on pavement parking and other pavement obstructions.

8.26 Penalties for certain driving offences including pavement parking should be increased.

A pleasant environment

Simply ensuring a satisfactory level of pavement maintenance will not, in itself, ensure that conditions for pedestrians are positively pleasant. A range of other measures—from preventing unpleasantness to designing fun and pleasure into the environment—are also needed. Although many of the individual measures are themselves simple, the overall task is a challenging one, and involves a range of actors including local authorities, the police, central government, voluntary groups and private firms.

(a) Preventing unpleasantness

Our first group of recommendations are primarily concerned with preventing those things that offend pedestrians. These include dog dirt on pavements, pavement cycling and obstructions on the pavement. We recommend that:

8.27 The best solution to the problem of dog dirt would be an extension of the experiments with local 'poop-scoop' schemes to other areas.

8.28 The police should also be more willing to enforce the law on pavement cycling. We understand the reluctance to force children to ride in the carriageway and would suggest that, until real progress has been made on the creation of cycle tracks, explicit local agreements could be reached to allow children under the age of ten to cycle on pavements (children below that age could not, in any case, be prosecuted).

8.29 Wherever possible, cycle tracks should be created by taking space from the carriageway, not the pavement. Only the widest pavements should be considered suitable for cycle tracks, and there should, ideally, be physical barriers separating cycles from pedestrians.

8.30 Unnecessary street furniture should be removed from the pavement. The remaining street furniture should be designed to be easily detected, even by the blind and partially sighted.

(b) Creating a pleasant environment for pedestrians

Pedestrians and motor vehicles have different requirements of their environment, and therefore require separate consideration. We have argued that designers and planners have given too much weight to the needs of vehicles, and that this imbalance needs to be redressed. This involves the formal planning system in decisions about the location of facilities, the design of details of street furniture, lighting and so on, and also the managers of shopping centres and other public spaces. We have argued that the key to this process is better consultation with the people who use the facilities provided. This process inevitably must involve a dialogue in which those with expertise both explain their plans and justify their decisions and also, where necessary, modify them in the light of consumer reaction. We recommend that:

8.31 District councils should prepare pedestrian movement plans, especially for urban areas. This would help to pinpoint particular problems such as long delays crossing roads or stretches of congested pavement. It would also be useful in creating networks of pedestrian zones, rather than isolated pockets, and would help in the strategic planning of future developments.

8.32 District councils should also carry out annual surveys to monitor particular problem areas.

8.33 Proposals for significant new developments should be accompanied by a pedestrian impact analysis, showing how the development would affect pedestrians both locally and further afield. These should be required, for example, of new shopping schemes, factories, hospital reorganisations and school closures or amalgamations.

8.34 Government should ensure that the needs of pedestrians are properly considered by local authorities in all the main planning documents— transport policies and plans, structure plans and local plans.

8.35 A design award for excellence in planning for pedestrians should be established.

Safety

We have seen that pedestrians are among the most vulnerable of road users. Pedestrians come off worst in accidents involving motor vehicles, but we have also shown in this report that the pavements themselves are responsible for a very much larger number of accidents.

(a) Preventing pavement injury

These accidents are neither recorded nor acknowledged, though a proportion of them are serious. The principal causes of these accidents are damaged pavements, and uncleared snow and ice. We have already made specific proposals for reducing pavement damage, and ensuring that damaged pavements are identified and repaired. Holes in the road are another perfectly avoidable source of danger. Weather conditions are clearly less tractable, but local authorities could, in our view, do more to minimise the risk to pedestrians during adverse weather. We recommend that:

8.36 *All public utilities and local authorities involved in streetworks should adopt the Horne Report's proposals on the signing, guarding and lighting of streetworks, and should ensure that the Report's recommendations on the enforcement of safety requirements are properly and fully adopted.*

8.37 *Precisely targeted publicity should be undertaken to remind pedestrians to take greater care during periods of hazardous weather conditions, perhaps by use of public-service broadcasts on local radio and television.*

8.38 *Householders should be encouraged to take responsibility for clearing snow and ice from immediately in front of their dwellings. Local authorities should provide sand and grit bins for this purpose.*

8.39 *The Department of Transport should undertake a detailed study of the frequency, seriousness, patterns and overall cost of pedestrian accidents caused by footway falls.*

(b) Road safety

The agencies, responsibilities and approaches involved in road safety matters are diverse and complex. The police, traffic wardens, surveyors, planners, engineers and road safety officers are the main actors dealing with safety. On specific occasions the public in general, or particular local communities, are also called upon to comment upon particular proposals. It needs ingenuity, a combination of approaches, technical skill, local expertise and public acceptance, for the conflicting demands of road users to be satisfactorily untangled.

The status of the police traffic safety function is thought to be too low by the officers both in the Metropolitan Police and ACPO with whom we spoke. Surveyors, planners and engineers appear to be locked into a highly departmental set-up in local government, often operating in different tiers of councils. Road safety officers, according to some observers, are given far too little authority, and too few resources.

We have already proposed the establishment of pedestrian units in local authorities, and we would expect them to play a major role in road safety. They could, for example, assist road safety engineers in undertaking a 'safety audit' at the planning and design stage of major new road or traffic management schemes, along the lines of schemes pioneered in Hertfordshire and the GLC. We believe that more could be done in terms of education, of engineering and of enforcement, and recommend that:

8.40 *The driving test should be reviewed to see if more emphasis could be placed on awareness of and ability to deal with the major conflicts that cause pedestrian accidents.*

8.41 *Consideration should be given to a 'probationary year' for new drivers, during which conviction for a driving offence would require retraining and perhaps retesting.*

8.42 *The police should adopt more passive devices—including cameras at traffic lights and radar warning notices—to deter illegal driving.*

8.43 *Consideration should be given to fitting cars with speed warning lights, to alert both the driver and the police that speed limits are being exceeded.*

8.44 *Drivers should be the target of far more specific education and publicity about their responsibilities towards pedestrians. This awareness should be incorporated into official guidance, such as the Highway Code and the 'Driving' manual.*

8.45 *Children and young people should receive comprehensive road safety education throughout their school years. This should not simply be confined to a small element of the formal school curriculum. For pre-school age children a national Traffic Club should be established along the lines of the Scandinavian and GLC/TRRL experience.*

8.46 *Local authorities should be required to produce an annual public report on their road safety initiatives undertaken over the year, including information from the local police committees on enforcement of traffic offences.*

8.47 *All local authorities should incorporate a 'safety audit' into their design of major traffic and highway schemes prior to implementation.*

8.48 *All local authorities should adopt the good practice of those with Accident Investigation and Prevention Teams.*

8.49 The official government regulations governing installation and operation of road humps, crossings and traffic light controls should be relaxed or amended to the status of guidance for councils.

8.50 As immediate priorities, council schemes should make maximum use of available engineering and traffic management measures to: slow traffic on residential roads; relieve street parking; create safe routes to schools; increase safe road-level crossing points.

8.51 The Department of Transport should review the transport supplementary grant, and its effect on the provision of resources for local road engineering and traffic management schemes aimed at reducing danger to pedestrians.

(c) Redress

Clearly, prevention of accidents is always preferable to a system of redress, however comprehensive. Nevertheless, accidents will continue to happen and it is important that the victims are not caused extra suffering by an insensitive and unresponsive system.

The National Consumer Council is critical of the present system of compensation for personal injury. This is an area outside the scope of this report, but aspects of it clearly relate to the unsatisfactory nature of redress for road and pavement accidents examined in chapter 3. In general, we believe that:

8.52 A simpler and quicker system for handling all personal injury claims is needed. This should include the introduction of a standard claim form and provision for the initiation of county court proceedings if no action has been taken by the relevant authority within a set period of time.

Time and again the courts express their sympathy for the victims of a pavement accident, accept that the victim was not to blame, and yet award no compensation. We believe that the definition of danger should be tightened. The defence of contributory negligence will allow the court to determine whether a given person took reasonable care of themselves bearing in mind the nature and existence of the danger. We would recommend that:

8.53 The test for a dangerous pavement should be based on whether the pavement would be a danger for any person, including infirm, elderly and disabled people. Once it is a danger to anyone, the duty to maintain should bite, and a failure to do so should give rise to a claim for damages where someone is injured.

While we accept that pedestrians like every other road user should and do take more care of themselves during snowy and icy periods, we feel the courts have taken too lax a view on the duties and priorities of highway authorities. People should not be housebound by bad weather, nor should they be forced to brave hazardous conditions entirely at their own risk. We recommend that:

8.54 The law should be changed to require highway authorities to make pavements safe from snow and ice as soon as is reasonably practicable and in any event at the same time as they made safe any other part of the highway.

Members of the public should be encouraged to report dangerous pavement conditions, to complain about accidents they suffer and, where appropriate, to claim compensation. We recommend that:

8.55 Local authorities, advice centres, hospitals and doctors should disseminate public information about legal rights and procedures for personal injury accidents, specifically including pavement accidents. Standard claim forms should be available through health centres, social clubs, day centres for the elderly etc.

8.56 The Motor Insurers' Bureau compensation scheme should be far more widely publicised. The police should send details as a matter of course to victims of hit-and-run accidents. Details should be readily available at health centres, hospitals and doctors' surgeries.

8.57 Local authorities and their insurers should be required to keep records of all highway claims, and details of their handling and the outcome of those claims. These records should be made publicly available.

8.58 Magistrates' courts should be encouraged to make full use of their powers to make compensation orders against motorists convicted of driving offences involving personal injury or other losses to victims, dependants or relatives.

Local action

We have argued that pressure for change needs to be applied to local government—pressure downwards from central government and pressure upwards from pedestrians and local people themselves.

Co-ordination is necessary to enable local groups to draw on examples of effective campaigning elsewhere, to help them work for change in their own neighbourhoods. We have shown in chapter 2 the extent of dissatisfaction with the present level of provision for pedestrians. There is, we believe, a great deal of potential support for campaigners about pedestrian issues. While few community groups or local branches of national organisations are concerned primarily with pedestrian matters, there are compelling reasons for putting them on the agenda for the first time or for giving them a higher priority—particularly for organisations concerned with the needs of elderly people, disabled people, women, children and the poor—all those who travel mostly on foot or for whom safety is a crucial issue.

Collective action will usually be more effective than action by the individual. Nonetheless, there are things that individual citizens can do. Both individuals and groups need to be able to gather evidence, assemble their arguments, recruit allies, and present their case with vigour, if they are to play a constructive role in improving local conditions.

Most importantly, they can monitor the state of the pavements and pedestrian facilities in their neighbourhood and inform the council when repair work is needed. We have seen that the more responsive councils already encourage feedback from the public through pre-paid postcard schemes; direct phone lines to complaints officers; regular public meetings, or public question-time slots at council meetings; co-option of representatives of pedestrian interests on to road safety, highways or police committees. Where such opportunities to participate exist, they should be used.

In all local authorities, pedestrians can make representations to their district or county councillors, or directly to the chairpersons of the relevant authority committees. They can make their views known when authorities consult on planning proposals. Finally, if they have a pavement accident, they can explore, perhaps with the help of an advice or law centre, whether they can claim for compensation with any chance of success.

The National Consumer Council believes that local campaigns on pedestrian issues are to be encouraged. We therefore recommend that:

8.59 *Pedestrians themselves should organise at a local level to analyse conditions for pedestrians in their area and to use the political process to communicate their concern.*

This last recommendation is one in which the National Consumer Council itself plays a direct role.

We are publishing an action guide—*Pedestrians*—as a complement to this report. The main aim of the guide is to provide local groups with expertise and a distillation of other people's campaigning experience. We hope thereby to help local people to contribute to their local authorities' plans; to make constructive proposals for improving conditions for pedestrians; and to work with those authorities who are receptive to the needs of pedestrians.

References to chapter 8

1. Standing Committee on Highway Maintenance, *National road maintenance conditions survey 1985, Report,* Department of Transport, 1986.
2. The Institution of Highways and Transportation, *Guidelines for providing for people with a mobility handicap,* IHT, February 1986 and Association of London Borough Engineers and Surveyors and Department of Transport, *Highways and traffic management in London, a code of practice,* HMSO, April 1986.

Appendix A
Research methods

To get an informal feel for the problems people encounter, we sent a press release to national and local newspapers asking people to write to us about their experiences—positive and negative—as pedestrians.

"Are your local pavements a delight to walk on? Are they kept free of litter and in good repair?

Or are they littered with Coke cans and beer bottles? Do parked cars, vans and lorries block your pavements? Do children use them as cycle tracks? Is dog dirt a problem? Are paving stones left unrepaired? Or—if you live in the country—is your problem simply that in your neighbourhood, there are very few pavements—leaving elderly people particularly at risk from passing traffic?

The National Consumer Council would like your comments on the pluses and minuses of being a pedestrian."

(12 July 1985)

Some local newspapers and radio stations made only a brief mention of our work, others used the release as the basis for a major piece. We received 536 letters and one package of dog dirt. The main problems people raised were the physical condition of pavements, obstructions, litter and dog dirt, cycling and driving on pavements, noise and particular hazards. Two groups were singled out for criticism: local authorities for their inaction on pavement repairs and maintenance and the police for not enforcing street offences. Just over one in ten of the letters told us about injuries and accidents sustained on the pavement.

Using this information and the results of an earlier (1979/80) Consumer Concerns study, we designed a questionnaire covering the journeys people make as pedestrians, the main problems encountered, views on safety and cleanliness of the environment, the incidence of pedestrian accidents and claims for compensation. Personal interviews were carried out for us by Market & Opinion Research International (MORI) in February 1986 among some 2,000 adults in Great Britain, as part of its regular omnibus survey.

To look at pedestrian accidents and claims for compensation in any detail required much larger sub-samples than could be obtained from an omnibus survey. We therefore placed a number of questions in Consumer Association's 'Supertrawl' survey in February 1986. This was a postal survey carried out among a random sample of 43,433 subscribers to *Which?* magazine. The section on pedestrian accidents was completed by nearly 28,000 people. The sample is not representative of the whole population, but the results turned out to be broadly compatible with those obtained from the MORI survey, and allowed us to look with more confidence at the experiences of those who had been involved in pavement accidents. A third survey was carried out with people who had reported having suffered pavement accidents, either directly to the NCC or to the Pedestrians' Association. Seventy-five people provided us with evidence about their injuries and any attempts they had made to claim compensation.

We also commissioned a number of papers from outside experts: on the administrative context of providing for pedestrians from Anthony Ramsay of Strathclyde University, on the law relating to pedestrians from Alec Samuels, and on the 'dog problem' from Astrid Klemz.

Because our aim was to produce an action guide for pedestrians, as well as the report itself, we tried to involve local voluntary groups in the research process. With Anthony Ramsay's help we designed a range of material including a physical survey of pavement defects and an interview questionnaire on pedestrians' concerns. These were piloted for us by Aberdeen Consumer Group, Adamsdown Community Law Centre (Cardiff), Age Concern Blackpool, Oxford Consumers Group, Newcastle Friends of the Earth, West Cumbria Community Transport, the Community Technical Aid Centre, Manchester and the Downland Group of the Wiltshire Federation of Women's Institutes. We also commissioned Transport and Environment Studies (TEST) to prepare a simple method for surveying local problems connected with crossing roads. This was piloted by the Aberdeen Consumer Group and comments were received from Friends of the Earth, Pedestrians' Association, Manchester Safe Routes to School Project and Barbara Preston for the Greater Manchester Transportation Consultative Committee. The pilots were invaluable in identifying design faults in our material.

To gain an understanding of the local authority viewpoint, we held discussions with the Association of County Councils, the Association of Metropolitan Authorities, the County Surveyors Society and the

Association of Chief Technical Officers (ACTO), the professional organisation for relevant officers in non-metropolitan district councils in
England and Wales. The Association of District Councils circulated a
note about our work to member councils, encouraging those with a
particular interest in pedestrians to send us details about plans and
developments. Some 63 councils wrote to us, often in great detail.
With ACTO's assistance, we drew up a questionnaire for district
councils seeking information about agency agreements, expenditure,
pavement inspections and enforcement, pedestrians' complaints and
problems, trips and falls on the pavement, and examples of good
practice.

Discussions with a very wide range of organisations and individuals
provided one of our major sources of information. As well as the local
authority and professional organisations mentioned above, we talked to
the Transport and Road Research Laboratory, officials at the Departments of Transport and the Environment, the Association of Chief
Police Officers, the Metropolitan Police, the Greater London Council,
the Pedestrians' Association, Friends of the Earth, Age Concern, the
Joint Committee on Mobility for the Blind, the National Paving and
Kerb Association, Terence Bendixson, and Dr John Adams.

We received evidence and information from an even wider range of
organisations, including the Association of London Borough Engineers
and Surveyors, RADAR, the Joint Committee on Mobility for the
Disabled, the Association for Neighbourhood Councils, the National
Federation of Women's Institutes, Pensioners' Voice, the Association
of Liberal Councillors, SPOKES (the Lothian Cycle Campaign), the
London Cycle Campaign, the National Association of Women's Clubs,
the National Housewives' Association, the Disabled Living Foundation,
and the London Planning Aid Service.

The report covers provision for pedestrians in England, Wales and
Scotland. Reluctantly we were forced to exclude Northern Ireland
because we lacked the resources to extend our investigation into
the province. The General Consumer Council for Northern Ireland,
however, is taking a particular interest in the needs of pedestrians and
will be giving evidence, in 1987, to a public inquiry into the Belfast
Transportation Strategy Review.

Appendix B
Who walks where?

Walking is an (almost) universal activity, as taken for granted as breathing, sleeping or eating and, like these other basic activities, it serves a vital function. Walking provides *mobility*, giving access to work, leisure, shops, medical and welfare services, and education.

Not everyone is equally dependent on walking, however. There are huge variations in the amounts and distances people walk, their reasons for walking, and the patterns and routes they use. These differences are closely linked to differing needs, lifestyles, and capacities. If there is an 'average' pedestrian, she is likely to be middle-aged, possibly infirm, and almost certainly lacking easy access to any alternative means of transport. But the National Consumer Council is not of the view that pavements should be designed for a mythical 'average person'. That would do no justice to the range of capacities within the population. We believe that provision should be based on the principle that anyone with the ability to be mobile on foot or by wheelchair should be able to get about with the minimum difficulty.

Walking: not quite universal

A minority of people cannot walk at all, or experience difficulties in walking, and yet need to get about. This includes the very young and a good number of the very elderly; people with some sorts of disability, and others more broadly defined as having a 'mobility handicap'.

A major survey of walking behaviour by the Office of Population Censuses and Surveys (OPCS), published in 1980 (1), found that two per cent of the total sample could not go out on foot. The proportion rose to eight per cent among those aged 70 to 79, and more than a quarter (28 per cent) of the over-80s.

Among the over-60s group, Todd and Walker found that seven per cent never went out on foot. A local study of elderly people in Guildford showed that 11 per cent of people over 65 had not been out in the past month, and that 44 per cent reported walking difficulties due to ill-health (2).

A large number of the elderly are also wheelchair-bound: of just under half a million wheelchair users in the UK, 86 per cent are above pensionable age.

Over 1.25 million adults between the ages of 16 and 65 are estimated to suffer from disability (physical, sensory or mental) (3). Some 70,000 are wheelchair users (4). For the severely physically disabled, the most important aid to getting about outside the home is private transport. For the majority of this group, however, walking difficulties can be enormously reduced through improved design and physical provision.

It is not only disabled people who have some form of mobility handicap. The Institution of Highways and Transportation put the number at ten million, including those who suffer temporary restrictions on the normal activities of life. People coping with children (with or without pushchairs or prams), carrying shopping or luggage, pregnant women, those who have had an accident like a broken leg—all encounter such restrictions.

This wider official definition of personal mobility handicap shows the huge *numbers* of people for whom walking is a less than straightforward matter. It also highlights the fact that the fittest of individuals may at some time fall into that group, if only temporarily.

Why do people make journeys on foot?

Far from being a leisure activity confined to rambling enthusiasts, walking is an essential day-to-day means of transport. One study estimates that between 27 and 45 per cent of all local journeys are made on foot (5), while another calculates that city or large-town dwellers walk or cycle 35 to 40 per cent of the time (6).

Not surprisingly then, walking is a significant means of transport in all types of journey, accounting for about one-fifth of journeys to and from work, nearly half of all shopping trips, one-third of social and personal-business trips (to banks, dentists, benefit offices, etc.), about two-thirds of children's journeys to school, and over a third of recreational and other journeys (7).

A survey on the detail of walking trips (8) has attempted to estimate how *far* people walk:

	Average distance walked per day (kms)
work or education	0.47
shopping (including personal business)	0.69
social or entertainment	0.44
walks or trips (for recreation)	0.19
other	0.14

Some three-quarters of all walking journeys are less than 1.6 km (1 mile) in distance (9). Clearly, then, walking is a very important means of transport for short, local purposes.

But it also plays a significant role in slightly longer journeys too, though this varies with age, sex and social class. Hitchcock and Mitchell suggest that in 15 to 20 per cent of all journeys, a walking 'stage' of more than 50 metres is combined with another mode of transport, such as bus, car, etc.(10).

Who does the walking?

".... High income, car-owning middle-aged men living in the suburbs do not walk much, while low-income, non-car-owning, young women living near town centres walk a lot." (11)

Men tend to walk less frequently than women, except among the elderly. On average, men walk 1.82 km daily, and women 2.04 km (12). The OPCS study found that men are slightly more likely to walk to work (13), but a London-wide travel survey in 1982 showed that women in the capital made nearly three times as many trips to work on foot as men (14). This same survey found that 25 per cent of all women's trips were for shopping. Moreover, on average women walk twice as far and cross twice the number of roads in shopping journeys as do men (15). The NCC's own survey of pedestrian habits found that women are almost twice as likely as men to shop for food by foot at least once a week. Women are also more likely to escort their children to school or playgroup: in the NCC sample, nine per cent of respondents did this at least once a week, and women accounted for three-quarters of this number. Men appear to reserve their energies for more social pastimes, being more likely than women to walk to a recreation/sports or social club, and accounting for 70 per cent of those walking to the local pub weekly or more often (16).

Age affects walking habits, as could be expected from our earlier observations about disablement among the elderly. The infirm elderly with walking difficulties are also relatively unlikely to use public transport or to own a car (see Table B.1). This means that, despite their problems with walking, this group still rely heavily on this way of getting around. So the OPCS study, for instance, showed that the amount men walk varies little with age. Women over 60 walk less far than other people, but spend the same length of time out walking as elderly men. The NCC survey found that nearly half of pensioners go out walking for recreation at least once a week. On the other hand a substantial minority, just under a third of people over 60 according to OPCS, do not leave their homes at all on an average day.

At the other end of the age range, children between the ages of three and fifteen years are the greatest walkers of all. According to Hillman and Whalley (17) they make more daily journeys by foot than any other age group, and walking accounts for half of all their journeys made. It is regrettable that little other survey research exists on children's walking habits.

Social class is also linked to walking behaviour. The 1975/6 National Travel Survey revealed that while 11 per cent of journeys to work by professional and managerial workers are on foot, this rises to 42 per cent for unskilled manual workers (18).

Using similar data, Hillman and Whalley found that, for lower-income households, walking accounts for twice the amount of their daily journeys as it does for high-income groups (19), but as they point

Table B.1 Means of transport used, according to age

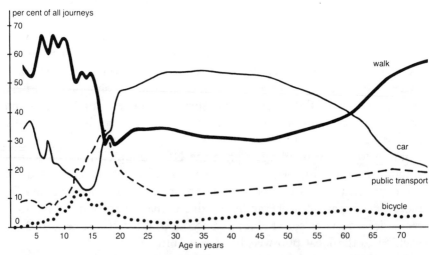

Note: this table is taken from *Walking Is Transport* by M. Hillman and A. Whalley (Policy Studies Institute, 1979) and is based on the 1972/73 National Travel Survey in which respondents gave their precise ages up to 20-years-old. Although somewhat out of date, the graph still usefully represents the *pattern* of journeys made by the various age groups.

out, the crucial factor is car ownership: better-off people are simply much more likely to own and use cars.

Some of the more extreme differences from NCC's survey are given in Tables B.2 and B.3. The difference in shopping behaviour between car owning and non-car owning households emerges clearly:

Table B.2 Main food shopping trips, variations by social class

How often on average do you walk from home to . . . ?	**Total average**	Car in household	Social class AB	No car household	Social class DE
	%	%	%	%	%
Main food shopping:					
1–2 days per week	**19**	13	14	32	25
Main food shopping: never	**52**	61	60	32	42

(Base: 2034)

Source: Market & Opinion Research International, *Pedestrians*, Q1, February 1986.

Table B.3 Work and leisure trips, variations by social class

How often on average do you walk from home to . . . ?	**Total average**	Car in household	Social class AB	No car household	Social class DE
	%	%	%	%	%
Place of work: never	**43**	51	48	27	36
Social, sport, recreation club: never	**54**	59	60	46	49
Leisure: never	**24**	21	18	30	28

(Base: 2034)

Source: Market & Opinion Research International, *Pedestrians*, Q1, February 1986.

There are other variables which may affect who walks where. For instance, country-dwellers do *less* walking than town-dwellers, even though some of the individual journeys are much longer. In more general terms, different localities provide variations in types of transport, which will clearly influence the significance of walking to the individual. Town planning and development trends are also increasingly affecting how, when and where people walk (20).

Despite the surveys referred to in this chapter, there is remarkably little solid information about pedestrian activity. This gap is most acute at local level, where the greatest potential exists for research into consumer needs, preferences and habits. Only when such research has been refined and developed both nationally and locally—with the full participation of those who do the walking—will the decision-makers have a proper basis on which to assess the relative priority of competing and conflicting transport needs. It is time the blank side of the balance sheet was filled in.

References to Appendix B

1. J.E. Todd and A. Walker, *People as pedestrians*, Office of Population Censuses and Surveys, 1980.
2. J.M. Hopkin et al., *The mobility of old people: a study in Guildford*, quoted from A. Hitchcock and C. Mitchell, 'Man and his transport behaviour. Part 2a: Walking as a means of transport', *Transport Reviews*, vol.4, no.2, 1984.

   S.W. Town, *The social distribution of mobility and travel patterns*, TRRL Laboratory Report 948, Transport and Road Research Laboratory, 1980.
3. Calculation is made from figures supplied in S.W. Town, *The social distribution of mobility and travel patterns*, TRRL Laboratory Report 948, p.4, Transport and Road Research Laboratory, TRRL 1980.
4. According to the Access Committee for England, an independent national organisation promoting physical access to the environment for people with disabilities.
5. S.W. Town, *op.cit.*
6. S.Potter, *Modal conflict at the mezzo scale*, Open University New Towns Study Unit, 1978.
7. See S.W. Town, *op.cit.* and E. Daor and P. Goodwin, *Variations in the importance of walking as a mode of transport*, GLC Research Memorandum 487, Greater London Council, 1976.
8. J.E. Todd and A. Walker, *op.cit.*, Table 6.2.
9. S.W. Town, *op.cit.*, p.3.
10. A. Hitchcock and C. Mitchell, *op.cit.*
11. E. Daor and P. Goodwin, *op.cit.*
12. J.E. Todd and A. Walker, *op.cit.*, Table 4.1.
13. *Ibid.*, p.25.
14. Director General's report, *Women and transport*, W188, to GLC Women's Committee, Greater London Council, April 1983.
15. J.E. Todd and A. Walker, *op.cit.*, p.25.

16. Market and Opinion Research International, *Pedestrians*, Summary report prepared for National Consumer Council, MORI, February 1986.
17. M. Hillman and A. Whalley, *Walking is transport*, Table III.2, Policy Studies Institute, September 1979.
18. National Travel Survey results quoted in S.W. Town, *op.cit.*, p.9.
19. M. Hillman and A. Whalley, *op.cit.*
20. See, for example, S. Potter, *op.cit.*

Further reading

For more detailed studies of the patterns of walking in the population, consult:

1. M. Hillman, I. Henderson and A. Whalley, *Transport realities and planning policy*, PEP, December 1976.
2. M. Hillman and A. Whalley, *Walking is transport*, Policy Studies Institute, September 1979.
3. J.E. Todd and A. Walker, *People as pedestrians*, HMSO, 1980.
4. C. Mitchell and R. Stokes, *Walking as a mode of transport*, Transport and Road Research Laboratory, 1982.

Appendix C
Case histories of local action

Action by an individual

For ten years, Mr Clifford Howell, a local representative of the Pedestrians Association in the county of Avon, has campaigned on pavement accidents and compensation. As well as circulating the Pedestrians Association's literature he has produced his own explanatory leaflets for local fall victims. The greater part of his energy, however, has been devoted to casework on behalf of accident victims:

"Those that come my way are usually the ones who do not know how to manage their claims and have no knowledge of dealing with the authorities.... I will send them forms and advise on any unusual aspects of their case; if they are local I will visit them; I have, on a couple of occasions, arranged medical examinations for them and I will draft or write follow-up letters for them".

In 1985 members of the public reported to Mr Howell 138 'hazards', of which 63 had involved accidents; Mr Howell himself reported 126 hazards. By the end of the year 75 of the hazards had been cleared as the result of his action.

He has also organised a local Pavement Week—to discourage pavement parking, and like all successful campaigners, he writes regularly to the local papers.

Collective action

Groups are able to press harder; to draw on local expertise to strengthen their case; and to make more effective use of campaigning strategies.

(a) A community group campaigns about pavement defects

Prompted by enquiries and complaints from local people who had tripped or fallen over because of the condition of the area's pavements, the Riverside Residents Group in Cardiff decided to highlight the problem and press their County Council to take remedial action. To gather evidence, the Residents Group conducted an opinion survey, in which they interviewed 304 people, and a pavement defects survey of 22 of the area's streets.

They discovered that 90 per cent of their sample of residents thought that the pavements were in a 'bad' or a 'very bad' condition; that 43 per cent of the sample had suffered an accident or some form of inconvenience (for instance, damage to clothes or footwear); and that the worst affected people were the elderly and those who pushed prams, pushchairs and wheelchairs. A report, simply but professionally produced and aptly illustrated with telling photographs of uneven, broken and cracked paving stones, and inadequate 'patch' repairs, set out their findings and recommendations and called for urgent action for the authorities.

The report was submitted to the County Council in early 1985 and the Riverside Residents Group met officers in September. As a result, the County Council agreed to draw up with the Residents Group a five-year repair programme for 25 streets in the area. The target for 1986 was four streets. The work is under way.

(b) Publicity

In 1985, Friends of the Earth London Road Safety Alert organised a well-publicised piece of direct action against pavement parkers. Cars parked on the pavement were leafleted with FoE London Road Safety Alert parking tickets. The registration numbers of the leafleted cars were recorded. A 'hit squad' then lifted those cars which remained parked on the pavement on to the road.

(c) Seeking allies

As we saw in chapter 2, older people in particular are likely to regard cyclists as a menace, because many of them ride on pavements. However, pedestrians and cyclists have similar needs and both can benefit from schemes which promote joint facilities that make cycling and walking easier and safer. There may be strong arguments therefore for the two lobbies to join forces, particularly because the cyclists' lobby is often the more active and better organised.

Spokes—the Lothian Cycle Campaign—has promoted the work of the Lothian and the Scottish Railway Path and Cycle Route Project, a Scottish Office and Manpower Services Commission-sponsored initiative aimed at turning redundant railway routes into paths for cyclists and walkers. The construction of an extensive network of off-road paths, totally segregated from motor traffic, is well under way in Edinburgh.

(d) The pavement and people with disabilities

Years ago, the National Federation of the Blind of the United Kingdom, launched the Give us Back our Pavement Campaign—an effort to educate the public on ways of helping blind and partially sighted people to have safer and cleaner pavements. The main element of the campaign was a series of leaflets and posters targeted at those who cause hazards—pavement parkers, pavement cyclists, the owners of gardens from which trees and shrubs overhang, dog owners whose dogs foul the pavements, shopkeepers whose awnings or displays obstruct the pavement. They have also organised a 'pavement day ' and a 'pavement week', the latter sponsored by the Department of Transport.

(e) Putting the community's views at public enquiries

Since 1976, the Brent Federation of Tenants and Residents Association has fought the Department of Transport's road-widening plans for a section of London's North Circular Road. Their report, *A Pedestrian Nightmare*, highlighted the danger for pedestrians with detailed information about the high traffic volume and speed, the increasing pedestrian accident rate, the narrowness of pavements, the inadequacy of the central reservation and the lack of sufficient pedestrian-crossing facilities.

A follow-up report argued for the integrity of a community torn in two by the North Circular's dense and fast-moving traffic flow and against the view of officials in the Department of Transport that the local people should accept the evolution of two separate communities in the area. They also vigorously defended their community at the local public enquiry into the Department of Transport's plans, by co-ordinating and printing submissions by local residents affected by the proposal.

In preparing their submissions, the Federation made sure that the planning enquiry formalities were observed, turning to the local community law centre for expert help.

(f) Forming joint watchdog bodies

For eleven years, the Greater Manchester Transportation Consultative Committee has provided a forum for discussion and consultation for public, private and voluntary organisations interested in the development of transport policies in Greater Manchester. The Committee is serviced by the local Council for Voluntary Service and presents collective views of members on all local transport issues, responding in particular to the local authority's annual statement of policy and objectives. It has a broad remit which includes pedestrian concerns— for example, during 1984/85 it sought stricter enforcement of parking restrictions from the Greater Manchester Council Police Committee in order to discourage pavement parking; consulted with the county legal officer about pedestrianisation proposals and the county engineer's department and the city planning department about traffic circulation proposals.

In 1984, the Sheffield Branch of the National Federation of the Blind set up the 'Causey Campaign' to deal with some of the problems which people in Sheffield were experiencing with pavements. A working party was formed made up of people representing a wide variety of pavement users, including mother-and-toddler groups, people with physical disabilities and elderly people, as well as people with visual problems.

With financial backing from the Urban Aid Programme, the Campaign organised a three-stage local survey into problems with pavements: street interviews in the centre of Sheffield; a small-scale postal survey; members of the working party took photographs of some of the worst problems encountered by respondents.

A report, 'The Causey Campaign', was produced, and as a follow up, the Campaign is organising a special 'trip' for councillors, officers and local MPs. They will be invited to brave some of the city's pavements blindfolded and with a white stick or in a wheelchair.

Printed for HMSO
by Hobbs the Printers of Southampton
(141/87) Dd0240355 C35 2/87 G3379